INCREDIBLE BASEBALL TRIVIA

MORE THAN 200 HARDBALL QUESTIONS FOR THE THINKING FAN

DAVID NEMEC
FOREWORD BY SCOTT FLATOW

SPORTS
PUBLISHING

Sports Publishing books may be purchased in bulk at special discounts for sales promotion, corporate gifts, fund-raising, or educational purposes. Special editions can also be created to specifications. For details, contact the Special Sales Department, Sports Publishing, 307 West 36th Street, 11th Floor, New York, NY 10018 or sportspubbooks@skyhorsepublishing.com.

Sports Publishing® is a registered trademark of Skyhorse Publishing, Inc.®, a Delaware corporation.

Visit our website at www.sportspubbooks.com.

10 9 8 7 6 5 4 3 2

Library of Congress Cataloging-in-Publication Data is available on file.

Cover design Tom Lau
Cover illustration: iStock.com

Print ISBN: 978-1-68358-232-8
Ebook ISBN: 978-1-68358-234-2

Printed in the United States of America

To my nephews Matt and Andrew Nemec

Table of Contents

Foreword by Scott Flatow

I first became aware of David Nemec's work when a friend gifted me with a copy of *The Absolutely Most Challenging Baseball Quiz Book, Ever* (1977). After I read the first few pages, it became apparent that the audacious title was justified. Although I already thought myself an expert, this book proved an education. The following spring, I bought Nemec's follow-up, *The Even More Challenging Baseball Quiz Book*. Somehow, Nemec had topped himself. Now I was convinced that these books could not have been written by one man due to their scope and inventiveness. David Nemec, I honestly believed, was a consortium of highly knowledgeable and creative individuals writing under a pseudonym.

However, five years later, I was proven wrong when a friend I subsequently made revealed that he knew Nemec personally. Nemec and I finally met in 1991, at the National Convention of the Society for American Baseball Research (SABR), held in

New York that year. I wrote the trivia competition and Nemec spearheaded a four-man team that defeated a daunting quartet of defending champions in the finals. He would go on to win many other team contests as well as SABR's first individual tournament in 1995. Since then, Nemec has continued to pitch his posers through contentious strikes, steroid scandals and league realignments. *Incredible Baseball Trivia* proves he has lost nothing off his fast one. In fact, it may be even hotter.

Nemec's unique ability to connect seemingly unrelated players across eras sets his trivia books apart from standard fare. For example: What links Frank Schulte, Willie Mays, Jimmy Rollins, and Curtis Granderson? Maybe you got that one cold, slugger. But who among the experts can reason out how unsung nineteenth-century infielder Jack Crooks and Ted Williams fit together?

The best trivia books not only ask you to match wits with the creator but enlighten and entertain as well. On that score, Nemec once again blasts a grand slammer into the upper deck. Take a healthy swing at these offerings:

Who had the highest OPS among qualifying batters that did not win the MVP Award that year? Would you believe he also posted the second highest OPS ever among non-MVP winners in another season?

How about naming the first player to hit at least 15 homers in a season in both the National League and the American League? You'll win plenty of online bets with this one.

Who was the first slugger to club four homers off four different pitchers in one game? He later clocked the first regular-season dinger for the New York Mets.

Who are the only two hurlers to garner multiple Cy Young Awards who are currently eligible for the Hall of Fame and untainted by suspected steroid usage but have not been enshrined and never will be? Can you name them?

Can you name the only pitcher in the Hall of Fame who collected all of his big-league wins after turning 30?

How about nailing the only hurler in the twentieth century prior to Sandy Koufax to fan at least 300 batters in back-to-back seasons?

All these treasures and more await you. So step up to the plate and take your best cuts against a lifetime's worth of Nemec's most crafty deliveries.

Scott Flatow is himself a multiple SABR trivia champion. He has written several baseball quiz books on his own and co-authored numerous baseball books with David Nemec, including six annual editions of *Great Baseball Feats, Facts & Firsts*, four team quiz books and *This Day in Baseball*. Flatow is a lifetime resident of Brooklyn, New York, and currently teaches elementary school not far from what was once Ebbets Field.

Introduction

First, I want to thank those who played a large hand in making this book possible: my editor Jason Katzman, Ev Cope, Al Blumkin, Dave Zeman, Rob Rafal, Tony Salin, Ken Samelson, Tom Zocco, and, above all, Scott Flatow, a longtime colleague who was kind enough to write the foreword. For all the statistics I've cited herein, Baseball-Reference.com is my source.

Incredible Baseball Trivia is my tenth book of this sort, beginning in 1977 with *The Absolutely Most Challenging Baseball Quiz Book, Ever.* For those who took me up on my challenge, if you scored well back then, you are a near certainty to top the charts once again. All the names and events you'll meet up within these pages should strike a familiar chord, and in many of the answers there will be a bonus usually not found in books of this sort. Additional material about their subjects that will often surprise you and drive you to learn even more about them and their singular feats or fizzles.

If you're a newcomer to my style of quizzing the audience, you are just as likely to do yourself proud. So long as you have the patience to puzzle out answers that you won't always have on the tip of your tongue. That's the real acid test. That's what sets apart the true superstars of baseball lore. Not a computer memory but a willingness to chomp on a few clues, a couple of seemingly disparate stats or odd record combinations, and soon enough make the connection between them.

Baseball. The game mesmerizes you. It is designed to mesmerize you. There is a vast kinetic quality to it, an ineffable romantic quality to its lore that in the end is what hooks you for life. For baseball, unlike football or basketball or hockey or indeed any of the other forms of entertainment that provide us with our cultural superheroes, has a built-in attraction to its all but bottomless tradition. There is a song featuring Van Lingle Mungo. Name one about a star in any other sport, let alone a good but hardly great player. Why is baseball rife with memorable nicknames like the Big Train, Stinky Stanky, and the Splendid Splinter whereas Jim Brown was never known by any name but Jim, Mario Lemieux any name but Mario, and George Mikan any name but George? How many sports-minded members of the general public who know Ty Cobb's career batting average and the significance of the number 714 also know Michael Jordan's career record for the most points per game or the NFL career record holder for the most touchdown passes prior to the merger of the NFL and the AFL in 1969? What do these team names, the Los Angeles Dons, the Miami Seahawks, and the Chicago Hornets have in common as opposed to the Chicago Whales, the Baltimore Terrapins, and the Brooklyn Tip-Tops? What team holds the record for the most points in a National Hockey League season as opposed to the most wins in a major-league baseball season? The true baseball fan has literally hundreds, even thousands of names, statistics, and anecdotes about his favorite game in his memory bank while died-in-the-wool fans in all other sports have far less. Why? What is the special magic that baseball and its names and numbers and tales hold?

There are many explanations for this phenomenon, but all agree on only one thing. It's undeniably true. *Incredible Baseball Trivia* is loaded with other sorts of mysteries about the game. Here's a sample. How could a team lead its league in batting average, fielding average and lowest ERA—in other words, win the team Triple Crown!—and yet finish no better than third? I have every confidence that you're up to solving this one and the vast majority of my other puzzlers. On each question just wait for your pitch—it'll come into your zone in due time—and then take it deep.

Oh, nearly forgot. Every section ends with a 5***** question that is guaranteed to contest your mettle even if you otherwise bat 1.000.

—David Nemec, Laguna Woods, California

Home Run Feats Throughout History

A FEW SOFT TOSSES
TO GET THE JUICES FLOWING...

*All of the current members of the 500 home run club were born
in the same century except one. Who is the only outlier?*

If you struggled here, you may be out of your depth. Babe Ruth
is, of course, the only current member of the 500 home run club
who was not born in the twentieth century. He was born in 1895.

*Who was the last slugger to join the 500 home run club before
the first wave of expansion occurred in 1961?*

Ted Williams in 1960. It would then be a while before Mays and
Aaron followed and after that came the deluge.

Name the five sluggers who smacked 500 or more career homers without ever striking out 100 times in a season.

In the order they did it: Babe Ruth, Mel Ott, Ted Williams, Hank Aaron, and by far the hardest and most surprising of the quintet—Gary Sheffield.

The last member of the St. Louis Browns to lead in the American League in home runs also holds the all-time season record for the most RBI at his main position.

In 1945, Browns shortstop Vern Stephens led the AL with 24 home runs, the last Brownie to do so. Four years later, after being traded to the Red Sox the previous season, Stephens notched 159 RBI, still the single-season record for a shortstop, and tied Ted Williams for the AL RBI lead. Stephens tied Red Sox teammate Walt Dropo in 1950 for the AL RBI lead with 144 and had earlier won an undisputed RBI crown as a member of the Browns' lone pennant winner in 1944. Honus Wagner, with four, is the only shortstop to win or share more RBI titles than Stephens, and not all of his wins came with him playing mainly at shortstop.

NOW THEY START TO GET TOUGHER...

All of the following batsmen except one enjoyed at least one season in which he led a Brooklyn–LA Dodgers team in home runs: Len Gabrielson, Gene Hermanski, Babe Herman, Hack Wilson, Shawn Green, Joe Medwick, Candy LaChance, Gil Hodges, Steve Garvey. Who is the only outlier?

You weren't paying attention in the 1960s if you guessed Gabrielson or in the 1890s if you bit on LaChance. Rather surprisingly, it's Joe Medwick, a Triple Crown Winner with the Cards, but little more than an average player by the time he was traded to the Dodgers after he sustained a serious beaning at the hand of Bob Bowman.

In the decade of the 1970s (1971–1980), only four American Leaguers hit as many as 40 home runs in a season, and none did it between 1971–1977. Two of the four are in the Hall of Fame including the decade dinger leader with 310. Name all four.

Jim Rice in 1978 with 46, Gorman Thomas in 1979 with 45, and Reggie Jackson and Ben Oglivie tied with 41 each in 1980. Jackson was the decade home-run leader with 310.

A post-2000 slugger rapped .196 after leading his league in home runs the previous year with a whopping total of 53. His 90-point drop in batting average is by far the greatest among American Leaguers in the season after they cracked the 50-homer barrier. The all-time record drop, though, still belongs to a National League slugger whose BA toppled 95 points after he posted his lone 50-homer season. Who were these two One-Year Wonder sluggers?

Orioles first baseman Chris Davis hit .196 in 2014 after leading the AL with 53 taters in 2013. He also hit .286 that year and hasn't come close since to matching that mark, dropping all the way to .168 in 2018. In 1931, the Cubs Hack Wilson hit just .261

after rapping .356 the previous year with a then NL record 56 home runs.

Name the only two players to hit five homers in a double header. Both did it with National League clubs, and the first of the pair accomplished the feat in 1954 and in a park based in the city where the only slugger to match his feat not only resided at the time but was at the park that day to witness this "Famous First!"

Stan Musial, in 1954 with the Cardinals at St. Louis's Sportsman's Park, a favorite haunt of eight-year-old St. Louis resident Nate Colbert, who would match Musial's feat 18 years later while with the San Diego Padres.

Who are the only two members of the Pittsburgh Pirates to compile as many as 35 homers in a season three or more times in Pirates garb?

If you said Ralph Kiner and Willie Stargell, you're only half right. Stargell had just two 35-homers or more seasons with the Corsairs. Kiner, on the other hand, had six and Brian Giles had four.

Who were the first two future Hall of Famers to homer in their first major-league plate appearances? Their big-league debuts occurred 23 years apart. Between them, they hit 239 home runs in regular-season play. All but one of those 239 homers belonged to the first of the pair to debut. The clues here will suffice if you know your Hall of Famers and their approximate debut years.

Earl Averill in 1929 and Hoyt Wilhelm in 1952. Wilhelm's seat finder was the lone four-bagger in his long career.

When the Great Strike shut down the 1994 season cold, freezing Ken Griffey Jr. (AL) and Matt Williams (NL) as the two league home run champs with 40 and 43 dingers, respectively, who was oldest living former league home run champ? His total for a full 154-game schedule in the year he led was less than either of the 1994 champs.

Dodgers first baseman Dolph Camilli led the National League with 34 homers in 1941. He was 87 years old when the season-ending strike occurred and died three years later at the age of 90.

Mark Teixeira holds the record for the most career grand slams by a switch-hitter with 12, but he is not the lone major leaguer to stroke a grand slam batting right-handed and left-handed in the same game. It was done in consecutive innings by a visiting player in Texas's Ballpark in Arlington. The player won a league batting title that same year.

But he never hit as many as 20 home runs in a season even though he belted three altogether on the day of his "Famous First." This feat occurred as recently as 2003, but already the perpetrator and his bat title that same season are all but forgotten. It was Bill Mueller, in his first season at third base with the Red Sox and by far his best year in the majors.

Who held the American League record for the most career home runs prior to the Babe's first 50+ home run season in 1920?

Shame on you if you thought it was the Babe himself. His 29 home runs in 1919 left him 31 homers short of Home Run Baker's total through 1919 of 80. Baker added to his total after 1919, but who noticed?

Who was the first slugger in major-league history to hit four home runs in a game in a losing cause? Can you also throw in the name of the rookie pitcher who on that day became the only hurler to rack up a complete-game loss despite receiving four-dinger support from a teammate?

The slugger was Phillies first baseman Ed Delahanty. At Chicago, on July 13, 1896, he tattooed right-hander Bill "Adonis" Terry for four dingers, accounting for seven RBI. But the Phils nonetheless lost, 9–8, when rookie Ned Garvin could not keep the Windy City crew in check. The game was a harbinger for Garvin, who always seemed to find ways to lose even when he pitched well, and he more often than not pitched very well. Apart from Delahanty, Bob Horner of the Atlanta Braves in 1986 was the only slugger to date to pound four homers in a losing effort.

Whose .260 batting average in a recent year is the lowest among all players who hit 50 homers in a season?

In 2010, the Toronto Blue Jays' slugger Jose Bautista broke Andruw Jones's 2005 mark of .263 for the lowest average by a 50-homer man when he went deep 54 times and hit .260. Bautista walked 100 times, however, giving him a .378 on-base percentage and leaving Jones still the record-holder for the lowest OBP (.347) among 50-homer hitters. Bautista's big year came out of nowhere. In none of his five previous major-league seasons had he ever hit more than 16 home runs, but he had several relatively strong seasons after that—along with some clunkers.

The lone slugger to knock 50 or more homers in a season and fan fewer than 50 times belted 359 dingers in his Hall of Fame career, but just once registered 50 or more strikeouts in a season. Who is he?

Johnny Mize in 1947 had just 42 Ks and 51 dingers. Prior to expansion in 1961, there were 13 seasons that featured a slugger with as many as 50 home runs and fewer than 100 whiffs. Since 1961, there have been just five such seasons, with Barry Bonds's 2001 campaign that included a record 73 homers and only 93 strikeouts the most surprising. Amazingly, Bonds fanned over 100 times just once, his rookie season in 1982 when he whiffed 102 times with the Pirates and hit just .223.

In Game 2 of the 2011 ALCS, Nelson Cruz of the Rangers belted the first walk-off grand slam home run in postseason history. Who, by rights, should the honor belong to instead, and why doesn't it?

On October 17, 1999, in the 15th inning of Game 5 of the National League Championship Series between the Braves and Mets in New York, Atlanta took a 3–2 lead in the top of the frame. The Mets, however, came storming back in the bottom of the inning and tied the game when catcher Todd Pratt drew a bases-loaded walk. That brought third baseman Robin Ventura to the plate. The lefty drilled a ball over the right-field fence off Braves right-hander Kevin McGlinchy for what should have been a game-winning, walk-off grand slam. However, as soon as the winning run crossed the plate, Pratt, who had been heading for second base, turned and raced back toward Ventura to hug him. Simultaneously, the Mets swarmed out of their dugout and onto the field to celebrate the victory. Since Pratt did not advance a base before Ventura passed him on the base paths, Ventura was credited not with a walk-off grand slam and four RBI but with just a walk-off RBI-single. It's known today as the "Grand Slam Single."

Five members of the 500 home run club wore only one team's uniform their entire careers. Name them and the uniforms they wore in the order they joined the club.

Mel Ott, New York Giants; Ted Williams, Boston Red Sox; Mickey Mantle, New York Yankees; Ernie Banks, Chicago Cubs; Mike Schmidt, Philadelphia Phillies. Narrow misses were Lou Gehrig with 493 home runs, all with the Yankees, and both Stan Musial and Willie Stargell with 475 homers, all with the St. Louis Cardinals and Pittsburgh Pirates, respectively.

The 500-homer club currently has only two members who were switch-hitters. Who are they, and who came the closest to becoming a third member before retiring with 468 home runs?

The two members are Mickey Mantle with 536 and Eddie Murray with 504. Chipper Jones currently ranks third among retired switch-hitters with 468.

What 500-homer club member broke into the majors as a shortstop, played one year as a regular at third base, won a batting title, played over 1,000 games in right field, and hit all of his four baggers with the following teams in the order

*named? Brewers, Padres, Marlins, Dodgers, Braves, Yankees,
Tigers, and Mets.*

Alex Rodriguez and Ernie Banks also played shortstop early on
in their careers, but neither played with teams in both leagues.
The answer is Gary Sheffield, currently the only player to drive
in 100 or more runs in a season for five different teams: Padres,
Marlins, Dodgers, Braves, and Yankees.

*Name the lone 500-homer club member who compiled fewer
than 2,000 career hits.*

Mark McGwire. Only twice did he log as many as 150 hits in a
season. In mid-career, he had the worst season by bat title qualifier of any 500 home run member when he hit a measly .201,
and in his final season he batted .187 in 97 games. McGwire's
strong links to steroid use eased the task of Hall of Famer voters
who might otherwise have been in a quandary about what to do
with a 500 home run club member (normally an all but auto-
matic ticket to admission) that possessed so few other qualities to
recommend his candidacy.

*Almost every eligible hitter of note during the decade of the
1930s (1931–1940) is in the Hall of Fame. But three sluggers
who hit 200 or more homers in that decade alone have yet to
make it. Who are they?*

Hal Trosky with 205, Wally Berger with 204, and Bob Johnson.
Johnson is the leader with 217 and also the only one with 2,000
hits and a .300+ career average. Johnson finished his career
in 1945 with the Red Sox after wasting his best years with a

miserable Philadelphia A's teams under Connie Mack. In 1936, Trosky, in the process of setting a new Cleveland season home run record of 42 that has since been broken, walked only 36 times to become the only pre-expansion player ever to hit as many as 40 homers and collect fewer walks than dingers. There have since been over a dozen.

For many years, until changes were made in its configuration, Washington's Griffith Stadium was arguably the hardest major-league park in which to go yard. Prior to 1954, only two members of the original American League Washington Senators had hit as many as 20 home runs in a season. Both did it in the same year but were best known for their slugging feats with other AL teams. Both hit right and were teammates that year of Goose Goslin, then in his final season and arguably the Senators' most prolific slugger prior to the 1950s. Who were they?

If you know Goslin's last season was 1938, chances are you also know the pair were first baseman Zeke Bonura with 22 jacks and a rapidly fading Al Simmons with 21. Park reconfigurations in the 1950s heavily favored right-handed hitters. First baseman Mickey Vernon was the only lefty to hit as many as 20 homers in a season with the AL Senators prior to expansion.

Even a modicum of knowledge of old ballparks should help you identify the last of the major-league parks that were built before 1925 and endured at least until expansion in 1961 to house a league home run king.

Yes, it was Comiskey Park. Bill Melton became the White Sox first home run king with a very modest total of 33 in 1971. Melton had also smacked 33 dingers the previous year but after 1971 never again knocked more than 21 blasts in a season. Somewhat bizarrely, after going 70 years without a home run king the White Sox had three in a four-year span as Dick Allen claimed their second AL home run crown the year after Melton's breakthrough and then won the crown again in 1974.

Who holds the single-season record for the most home runs in one major-league city?

You'd think it had to be New York, but no. Aaron Judge gave the record a serious challenge in his extraordinary rookie season in 2017 before falling short. But Judge broke the ancient and prestigious single-season record for the most home runs in New York City with 34. The previous NYC mark was 32, set by Babe Ruth in 1921. The record for any city belongs to Hank Greenberg, with 39 home runs in Detroit's Briggs Stadium in 1938. That same year, Jimmie Foxx set the current Boston record with 35 home runs in Fenway Park.

For well over half a century Frankie Frisch was believed to have been the first switch-hitter to collect 100 career home runs, but historians now know he was not. The first switch-hitter to do it threw left in his rookie season and hit exclusively from the right side of the plate. He also probably had seasons when he swung mainly from the left side of it. Though it remains to be discovered if he was the first to homer from both sides of the plate in the same game, it is definite that he was the all-time career home run leader prior to the Babe's arrival. Who is he?

Roger Connor, who was not officially acknowledged to have been a switch-hitter until 2017 after this book's author, among others, campaigned that there was just too much compelling evidence that he batted both ways.

What 500-homer member went yard more times before he turned 21 than he did after his 35th birthday?

It should immediately be clear that the answer here will not be a pre-free agency player since careers now, particularly among power hitters who can convert to DH in their later years, last much longer in large part because the money to be made is so much greater than it was when the Mantles and Aarons played. It is Mel Ott, who had 61 home runs before his 21st birthday and only 48 after he turned 35.

Who held the career record prior to 1924 for the most home runs by a righty? The only clues you should need is that he was the first rookie to be a league home-run leader and also the owner of the career record for the most home runs in the American Association.

Harry Stovey retired in 1893 with 122 home runs. His righty record was broken in 1924 by Rogers Hornsby, but he holds a more significant record that will almost certainly never be broken: the most games played (1,486) by a sub-.300 career hitter who scored more than one run per game (1,492). Stovey's .288 career batting average and failure to reach 2,000 hits (1,769) have kept him from Hall of Fame consideration in recent years, but the consensus among those who saw him play and were still alive when the Hall first opened its doors was that he belongs.

Who retired not long ago with 462 career home runs and never had a season in which he compiled more hits than strikeouts?

Adam Dunn with 2,379 Ks, 1,631 hits, and a .237 BA. Just once, in 2004, did Dunn log as many as 150 hits (151) in a season. Over a third of his hits (35.3 percent) were home runs. To his credit, Dunn walked 1,317 times and registered 100+ walks on eight occasions during his 14-year career.

Early in the 2010 season, Albert Pujols broke the record for most home runs in the first ten seasons of a big-league career with 408. Who held the previous record with 370 homers over the first 10 years of his career? He played with teams in five different cities and two different leagues but played for only three different franchises.

Eddie Mathews, a member of the Braves while they were based in Boston, Milwaukee, and Atlanta before joining the NL Astros and AL Tigers in 1967.

Who is the only major leaguer to steal 50 bases and swat 50 homers in a season in the same decade? He briefly held the American League record for the most consecutive stolen bases without being caught (36) before it was broken later that same year by Tim Raines and now belongs to Ichiro Suzuki (with 45 in 2007).

Baltimore center fielder Brady Anderson swiped 53 bases in 1992; four years later he popped 50 homers, most of them while batting leadoff. Anderson also holds the records for leading off the most consecutive games with a home run (4) and owning the fewest career home runs (210) by a retired player who clubbed 50 or more in a season. Even though he collected 110 RBI in his 50-homer season, he does not hold the season record for the most RBI by a leadoff hitter because he did not always bat leadoff in 1996, his 50-homer season. The record is held by the Rockies Charlie Blackmon with 104 in 2017.

Nowadays this feat is almost commonplace, but prior to 1991 it had never been done. That year, who became the first slugger to hit as many as 20 home runs while carrying a sub.-200 batting average?

In 1991, Tigers outfielder Rob Deer hit 25 home runs despite batting just .179. He finished with 230 career home runs and a .220 batting average, the lowest among sluggers with as many as 200 career home runs.

Before expansion in 1961, only one player in all of major-league history had tagged as many as 10 home runs in a season on a sub-.200 average. The following year, that same player became the only batsman in major-league history to smack four home runs in a game despite compiling fewer than 400 at-bats in his banner season. Who is he?

In 1947, Indians outfielder Pat Seerey collected 11 four baggers on a .171 batting average and just 216 at-bats. Traded to the White Sox early the following year, Seerey hit four home runs on July 18, 1948, at Shibe Park in the White Sox' 12–11 win over the A's in 11 innings with his fourth blast, in the top of the 11th off A's starter Lou Brissie (who entered in the ninth in relief), spelling the difference. But he was eventually benched that season because he fanned 102 times in just 363 at-bats, making him the only hitter prior to expansion to notch a three-digit strikeout total with fewer than 400 at-bats.

Only four players have won home run crowns in both the American and National leagues. There was a lapse of 84 years between the second and third men to achieve this feat. The first to do so began his career as a pitcher, and the achievements of the fourth and most recent slugger to accomplish it are tainted.

The first was Buck Freeman who led the NL in 1899 with the Washington Senators and the AL in 1903 with the Boston Americans; next to do it was Sam Crawford, who topped the NL with the Reds in 1901 and the AL with the Tigers in 1908. Fred McGriff led the AL in 1989 with the Blue Jays and then after an 84-year hiatus joined Freeman and Crawford when he led the NL with the 1992 Padres. The tainted feat belongs to Mark McGwire, the AL leader in 1987 and 1996 with the Oakland A's and the winner of back-to-back NL titles in 1998 and 1999 with the Cardinals.

Carlos Beltran's final career home run came on August 16, 2017, as a member of the Astros and made him only the sixth player to hit 200 or more homers in both the American League and National League. Who were the previous five?

In order, they were Frank Robinson (243 in the AL and 343 in the NL), Mark McGwire (363 in the AL and 220 in the NL), Fred McGriff (224 in the AL and 269 in the NL), Ken Griffey Jr. (420 in the AL and 210 in the NL), and Vladimir Guerrero (215 in the AL and 234 in the NL).

Forewarning: This one is much more difficult than it may appear. Who was the first player to hit as many as 15 home runs in a season in both the NL and AL?

Sam Crawford comes first to many historians' minds, but while Crawford hit exactly 15 homers in 1901 for the Reds in the NL, he never posted a double-digit home run total again after he joined the AL Tigers the following year. Buck Freeman is another good guess, but also wrong. The answer is a slugger who took the reverse route from Crawford, logging several double-digit dinger seasons with the Tigers before joining the Reds near the tail end of his career and banging 19 homers for the Crosley occupants in 1929: Harry Heilmann.

Wes Ferrell holds the career record for the most home runs by a pitcher with 38. Who is the only other player among the top five in home runs by a pitcher that is not in the Hall of Fame? He is also the last hurler among the top five to still be active as late as the 1970s.

Earl Wilson, in fifth place with 33 career dingers; he also hit two as a pinch hitter for 35 total.

In 1982, who became the first player since the mound was moved to its present distance in 1893 to win three home run crowns as a member of three different teams when he topped the AL by pasting 39 dingers for the Angels?

Reggie Jackson, also a leader with the A's and Yankees. Prior to 1893, Harry Stovey paced the NL in 1880 as a rookie with the Worcester Ruby Legs and again in 1891 while with the

Boston Beaneaters. In 1883 and 1885, he topped the American Association as a member of the Philadelphia Athletics and also tied for the AA lead in 1889 while still with the Athletics.

Who broke Earl Averill's career record for the most home runs in a Cleveland uniform when he racked up his 227th career homer the year before leaving the Tribe?

Albert Belle. He collected 242 career homers before leaving Cleveland to join the White Sox.

The first slugger to hit four home runs in a game off four different pitchers belted the first of his quartet off a Hall of Famer in the second inning. The remaining three were surrendered by Normie Roy in the third, Bob Hall in the sixth, and Johnny Antonelli in the eighth, respectively. Twelve years later, he hammered the first jack by a member of the New York Mets. Can you name both him and the Hall of Famer who was his first victim in his four-homer game on August 31, 1950?

The game occurred in Brooklyn's Ebbets Field between the Dodgers and Boston Braves. Warren Spahn started for the Braves and exited soon after serving up Gil Hodges's first of four circuit blasts. The only Braves pitcher to escape unscathed was Mickey Haefner. Because the Dodgers won the game handily, they did not bat in the bottom of the ninth, denying Hodges a chance for a fifth homer that day.

Even though he never hit as many as 40 home runs in a season, he collected 493 career round-trippers, the most by any indisputably eligible slugger not in the Hall of Fame and tied with Lou Gehrig for the most jacks by a player who fell short of joining the 500 home run club. Name him.

The Crime Dog—Fred McGriff. In 1994, McGriff was having what perhaps would have been the finest year of his career when the strike hit. He already had 34 homers and seemed a near cinch to top the 40 mark. Had the season played out and McGriff had logged just seven more homers to give him 41 he would have finished with 500 on the nose and would almost certainly now have a plaque in Cooperstown.

5***** John Clarkson retired in 1894 with the career lead in both home runs hit by a pitcher (24) and home runs surrendered by a pitcher (160). His former record fell by the end of the nineteenth century to Jack Stivetts, but his most career homers surrendered mark stood for over 30 years before finally being broken in the late 1920s by Pete Alexander. It has since been broken many times over. At one point, it was broken in back-to-back seasons by two pitchers who were both members of the Cleveland Indians when they gave up their record-breaking home runs. One won over 200 games, and the other coughed up 21 dingers in just 134 innings in his final season, spent on the same staff with a rookie fastballer who became the first pitcher since 1936 to be a first-ballot Hall of Famer. One last clue: Both record-setting hurlers died prior to expansion. You need both career home run record setters and the 'Famer to collect all five stars.

The record setters were George Blaeholder in 1936 and Earl Whitehill in 1937. Blaeholder's rookie phenom teammate was Bob Feller.

Major Award Winners

Who is the only player to win multiple MVP awards, none of which came while he was playing for a team with a winning record?

Chicago Cubs shortstop Ernie Banks was selected the National League MVP in both 1958 and 1959. In 1958, the Cubs finished tied for 5th place in an eight-team league with the Cardinals; the following year they again tied for 5th place, this time with the Reds. In both years, they had a losing record. During that same decade, in 1952, the Cubs finished alone in 5th place, 10 games behind the 4th place Phillies, but Chicago outfielder Hank Sauer nonetheless was voted the NL MVP for leading the league in RBI and tying Ralph Kiner for the home run crown on the strength of a rather pedestrian .270 BA and .892 OPS. Meanwhile, Robin Roberts, with 28 wins for the 4th place Phillies, the most victories by an NL pitcher since Dizzy Dean's 28-win season in 1935, finished a distant 2nd in the MVP balloting. No other team has ever had three MVP winners in a decade in which it never finished in the first division. There's just something about the Cubs. In 1987, despite finishing last in the NL East, they garnered yet another dubious MVP when Andre Dawson had a Sauer-type season, leading the league in homers and RBI but with otherwise undistinguished batting stats.

What player made his first starting appearance of the season in his lone BBWAA MVP Award–winning campaign in Game 1 of a World Series?

This question can be framed in about twenty different ways. Clearly, an MVP making his first starting appearance of the season in Game 1 of a World Series has to be a pitcher as opposed to a position player and, moreover, a relief pitcher. Because he was a relief pitcher, he at one time owned the record for the most mound appearances in a season at the 60-feet-6-inches distance with 74. That record was set in his MVP season. In his multiple-record season, he was not only the first reliever to win an MVP Award but also the first MVP to wear glasses on the playing field. The answer, should anyone still need it, is Jim Konstanty in 1950. Konstanty not only started Game 1 of the Series for the Phillies against the New York Yankees but hurled a 1–0 loss to Vic Raschi. It was his lone Series start, but he appeared twice in relief—again to no avail—as the Phils were swept, though it was the most competitive sweep in World Series history. Three of the Phils' losses were by a one-run margin. Konstanty remained a useful pitcher for several more years and in 1955 again qualified for the postseason as a member of the flag-winning Yankees.

Although he made 45 appearances during the regular season (all in relief) and had a 7–2 record and 12 saves, he was not used by Yankees manager Casey Stengel in the World Series.

Name the only player to receive votes for a Chalmers Award, a league MVP, and a BBWAA MVP. No fluke here, he finished in the Top 10 at least once in all three contests despite scoring 100 runs in a season just once, that with the 1922 Pirates.

Rabbit Maranville, the owner of a .658 career OPS and an 82 OPS+, both of which are the lowest among Hall of Famer position players (catchers excepted) who earned plaques solely for their playing accomplishments. In 1914, he hit just .246 but finished 2nd only to his fellow Boston Braves keystone partner Johnny Evers in the voting for the NL Chalmers Award.

Who won a Rookie of the Year Award and finished 4th, 2nd, and 6th in MVP balloting in his first three major-league seasons and 2nd in his 7th campaign but has yet to receive serious consideration for the Hall of Fame irrespective of his three batting titles? He played his entire career with the same team and under his brother's first name.

Tony Oliva, whose real first name is Pedro. A Cuban native, Oliva used his brother's birth certificate to enter the United States illegally. A severe knee injury when he was still in his prime restricted him to a DH role in his last four seasons and shaved about 10 points off his career batting average. Oliva had the further misfortune of playing his entire career not only with Minnesota, a small-market team, but in an extremely pitcher-friendly era.

Since the inception of MVP Award in 1931, who holds the record for the highest season OPS (1.287) by a non-MVP winner?

Ted Williams, in 1941, when he lost the award to Joe DiMaggio. Williams also had the second highest OPS by a non-winner (1.257 in 1957) when he finished second in the balloting to another Yankee, Mickey Mantle.

Who are the only two multiple Cy Young Award winners that have been eligible for the Hall of Fame for a number of years but are not as yet enshrined and are extreme longshots ever to be?

Bret Saberhagen won the Cy Young in 1985 and again in 1989 but had only one other season in which he won more than 14 games. Denny McLain garnered his first Cy Young in 1968 after becoming the AL's first 30-game winner since 1931; the following year he tied the Orioles' Mike Cuellar for the honor when each collected 10 of the 20 first-place votes. McLain's career after that became a living nightmare that included a 20-loss season and prison time.

Who is the first AL player to win the World Series and earn MVP, Gold Glove, and Silver Slugger Awards in the same season?

Mookie Betts, in 2018. The only NL player ever to do that is HOFer Mike Schmidt with the 1980 Phillies.

What middle infielder copped an AL MVP Award and missed being a unanimous winner by just one first-place vote in the last year that he received so much as a single vote in MVP balloting? Of the 20 ballots cast in his winning year, the only first-place vote that did not come his way went to a teammate.

In 1965, after the Minnesota Twins unseated the Yankees (who were shooting for a record sixth straight pennant), Twins shortstop Zoilo Versalles, a respectable but hardly impact player in his previous six big-league seasons, stepped forward to top the AL in runs, doubles, triples, and total bases. He also paced the AL in batters' strikeouts, hit just .273, and had an undistinguished .950 fielding average while leading the league in errors. Only teammate Tony Oliva's single first-place vote prevented him from being the junior circuit's unanimous MVP. In 1966, Versalles slipped to a .249 BA, and two years later, in his final season as a starter, he hit .196. A hematoma on his back accounted in part for his stunningly abrupt decline after 1965, but Bill James has noted that Versalles has the fewest career win shares (134) of any player ever to win an MVP Award (18) and only once prior to 1965—in 1962, when he got eight votes—was he even so much as mentioned for the award.

Who finished a mere fifth in his league's initial MVP Award voting in 1931 despite leading his loop in OPS and driving home 162 runs?

What's more, he hit .373 and logged a 1.195 OPS with 149 runs and five stolen bases. Yes, it's Babe Ruth. Finishing ahead of the Bambino that year were Lefty Grove, Lou Gehrig, Al Simmons, and Earl Averill. In the sixth slot was Earl Webb of the lowly Red Sox who was coming off a season in which he set the all-time record for doubles with 67.

Several teams have had only one Cy Young Award winner, and some have still never had one. What club saw four of its hurlers win a Cy Young in the 12-year period between 1969 and 1980, with one of the four winning it three times?

The Baltimore Orioles. In 1969, lefty Mike Cuellar shared the award with Detroit's Denny McLain. Jim Palmer won it outright three times: 1973, 1975, and 1976. Mike Flanagan took home the trophy in 1979, and the following year, Steve Stone bagged the honor after going 25–7. Stone's stunning season was followed by a dreary 4–7 ledger and a pink slip. Apart from Sandy Koufax, who retired voluntarily after winning the 1966 Cy Young, Stone's departure from the majors was the swiftest following a Cy Young triumph.

Who received just one vote the first year he appeared on an MVP Award ballot but swept the honor the next two seasons to become the first repeat winner?

Philadelphia A's first baseman Jimmie Foxx collected just a single vote in 1931 when he hit .291 with 30 homers. He took home the hardware for the first time the following year after hiking his dinger total to 58 and became the first repeat MVP honoree in 1933 when he bagged his first batting title and also won the Triple Crown. Foxx nearly won a second Triple Crown five years later when he won both another batting title and RBI crown but instead became the first 50-homer slugger to fail to lead his league in circuit blasts as Detroit's Hank Greenberg ripped 58 homers.

When Carl Yastrzemski won the 1968 American League bat title with a record-low .301 average after winning the Triple Crown and an MVP Award the previous year, the 1968 MVP Award rightfully went to 30-game winner Denny McLain of the Tigers. But two other pitchers and no less than five position players also received more MVP votes than Yaz did. Three of the five position players were members of the pennant-winning Tigers and one was a teammate of Yaz's. Can you name the four? Bravo if you also know the fifth and the two other pitchers who made Yaz settle for the ninth spot on the final list.

Ken Harrelson was Yaz's Red Sox teammate; Willie Horton, Dick McAuliffe, and Bill Freehan were the three Tigers' position players, with Freehan second only to McLain in the voting. Frank Howard of the Senators was the fifth position player, and the other two pitchers were the Orioles' Dave McNally and the Indians' Luis Tiant.

What pitcher won an MVP Award for a team that was 55–68 in games in which he did not get a decision?

In 1952, Bobby Shantz almost single-handedly brought respectability to the Philadelphia A's, leading them to their final first division finish when he went 24–7. A control pitcher, the diminutive (5-foot-6) lefty finished 27 of his 33 starts and led the American League not only in wins but in WHIP and fewest walks per 9 innings. However, his 279 ⅔ innings pitched took a heavy toll. Just once in his 13 remaining seasons did he appear in enough innings to be a qualifier.

The 2000 National League Rookie of the Year winner was the only position player who received ROY votes in the final year of the twentieth century and was still active as late as 2014. But an Oakland pitcher who received Rookie of the Year consideration in the American League in 2000 mounted a brief and rather embarrassing comeback with his original team a year later in 2015. Who were these two 2000 rookie standouts?

Rafael Furcal, the 2000 National League Rookie of the Year, was the lone 2000 rookie position player in either league to appear in the majors as late as 2014 after missing the entire 2013 season. But pitcher Barry Zito of the Oakland A's, who finished in a tie for sixth place in the 2000 AL ROY balloting, tried to return to the majors with the A's in 2015 after missing the 2014 season. Zito had suffered seven consecutive disappointing years with the Giants following his free agency acquisition from the A's prior to the 2007 campaign (going 63–80 with a 4.62 ERA). His comeback attempt in 2015 lasted all of seven innings in which he compiled a horrendous 10.29 ERA and 2.57 WHIP.

Who are the only two pitchers to bag four consecutive Cy Young Awards? Not surprisingly, both are in the Hall of Fame and won over 300 games.

Greg Maddux won four straight Cy Youngs in 1992–1995, the first with the Cubs and the last three with the Atlanta Braves. Randy Johnson, the oldest pitcher to win his first Cy Young Award (and go on to win multiple Cy Youngs), was thirty-five when he started his four-year CYA skein in 1999 with the Arizona Diamondbacks. Johnson also became the most recent Cy Young winner to collect three wins in a World Series when he led the Diamondbacks to victory over the Yankees in 2001.

In 1983, both Cy Young Awards went to previously unheralded pitchers on division winners, but only one of them pitched in the World Series that year. Between them, they logged just 221 regular-season wins, and both finished their careers with National League clubs in separate divisions. Who are they?

LaMarr Hoyt and John Denny. Denny finished with the Phils, his flag-winning team in 1983, and Hoyt, a member of the White Sox in 1983, last appeared with the 1986 Padres. By then both his career and life were in flames. He was arrested several times for drug possession and did time in prison.

Name the only middle infielder to win Rookie of the Year honors and finish among the top three in his league's MVP balloting in that same season.

In 2016, Dodgers shortstop Corey Seager was a unanimous pick for the National League Rookie of the Year. Seager also finished a strong third in the MVP voting behind the winner, Cubs third baseman Kris Bryant, and Washington second baseman and runner-up Daniel Murphy. It was the first time in history that the top three finishers in a league MVP race were infielders at three different positions and none was a first baseman. Note that not all authorities consider Seager to have been a rookie in 2016 since he had well over 100 plate appearances in 2015.

The Chalmers Award was first given to the player in each league chosen by a commission of baseball writers (one from each city in each league) as "the most important and useful player to his club and to the league at large" in 1911 and lasted four years. The rules stipulated that a player could only win the award once. All four of the American League selections are in the Hall of Fame. But the first three Chalmers Award winners from the National League are not and the fourth, second baseman Johnny Evers of the 1914 Boston Braves, is a somewhat controversial choice for the Hall. Who are the three NL Chalmers Award–winners that do not have a plaque in Cooperstown?

Cubs outfielder Frank Schulte won in 1911, Giant second baseman Larry Doyle received a new Chalmers automobile in 1912, and Brooklyn first baseman Jake Daubert got his in 1913. Schulte and Doyle were on pennant winners, but Daubert's sole credential was that he won the NL batting title in 1913 with a .350 average. Brooklyn meanwhile finished in 6th place.

In its first 11 seasons after being designated a major award (1956–1966), only one Cy Young Award was given each season. Of the first 11 Cy Young recipients, four are not in the Hall of Fame. One of the four also won his league's MVP trophy in his Cy Young season and was on a pennant-winning team. A second performed brilliantly in that fall's World Series, winning Game 6 and earning a save in Game 7. A third was also on a World Series victor the year he won the award. The fourth was the only winner between 1956–1966 who was neither on a World Series entrant nor a team that lost a pennant playoff series, as did Don Drysdale in 1962. Who are the four?

Don Newcombe of the 1956 Dodgers was also the NL MVP, Bob Turley of the 1958 Yankees, Vern Law of the 1960 Pirates, and Dean Chance of the 5th place 1964 Angels who led the AL in ERA and tied the White Sox Gary Peters for the lead in wins with 20.

The first team to win three consecutive MVPs, each by a different player, did it in the 1930s (1931–1940). Two of them are also the first two MVP winners who have yet to make the Hall of Fame. What is the team, and who were its three consecutive MVPs?

Cincinnati, with Ernie Lombardi (1938), Bucky Walters (1939), and Frank McCormick (1940). Until Lombardi was inducted into the Hall of Fame by the Veterans Committee in 1986, the 1939–1940 Reds were the only back-to-back pennant winners in either the National or American League that did not have a single major contributor with a plaque in Cooperstown.

Among position players that have won Rookie of the Year honors since the award's official inception in 1947, who are the only two that compiled more than half their major-league career hits in their award-winning seasons?

In 1962, Chicago Cubs second baseman Ken Hubbs was named the NL Rookie of the Year after he logged 172 hits, combined with a .260 BA. Hubbs played only one more season and finished it with 310 career hits to that point before dying prior to the 1964 campaign in a private plane crash. Some 28 years later, Cleveland unveiled a twenty-five-year-old yearling outfielder named Joe Charboneau who soon earned the nickname "Super Joe" for his feats on the playing field and "Bazooka Joe" for his bizarre behavior off it. Among other things, he opened beer bottles with his eye socket and drank the contents through a straw inserted in his nose. Nonetheless, an .846 OPS emanating from a .286 BA and 131 hits brought him the AL ROY. Soon thereafter, unlike Hubbs, who literally crashed and burned, Charboneau did so only figuratively. He left the majors with just 172 career hits and the fewest games played by a position-playing ROY winner, with 201.

In the first decade of the twenty-first century, who rudely interrupted Johan Santana's bid to become only the third hurler to win three consecutive Cy Young Awards when he collected 21 wins with an uninspiring 3.48 ERA in a year when Santana led the AL in WHIP, strikeouts, ERA+, and FIP?

After winning the Cy Young in 2004, Santana won again in 2006. But in 2005 the award went to the Angels' Bartolo Colon, who led the AL in wins only. Santana actually finished 3rd in the voting, trailing Yankees closer Mariano Rivera, in large part because he collected only 23 decisions in his 33 starts, giving him a 16–7 record, while Colon in the same number of starts pitched fewer innings and had fewer complete games but was credited with 29 decisions and a 21–8 record.

Who was the first starting pitcher in both the AL and NL to bag Cy Young honors despite failing to pitch a complete game all season?

Roger Clemens won the AL Cy Young Award with the Yankees in 2001 without a complete game, the first starter in history to do so. Three years later, by then with Houston, he became the first NL starter to make the same boast.

In 1999, Randy Johnson of the Arizona Diamondbacks received the NL Cy Young Award with a 17–9 record, beating out Mike Hampton of the Houston Astros, who went 22–4. What stat did Johnson own that enabled him to surmount Hampton's vastly superior W–L record?

Johnson hurled 12 complete games in becoming the last Cy Young winner to date with 10 or more.

How many post-1930 MVP Awards did Hack Wilson, Rogers Hornsby, Gabby Hartnett, Al Simmons, Babe Ruth, Pie Traynor, and Pete Reiser win combined?

Hope you didn't bite on Reiser. He was beaten out by teammate Dolph Camilli in 1941. The only one on this list to win an MVP was Hartnett, in 1935. All of the others except Traynor won a pre-1931 MVP Award.

Who was the first DH to win an MVP Award?

Don Baylor of the Angels, in 1979. It was a bizarre year for the MVP, as for the only time in history a league, the NL had co-recipients—Willie Stargell and Keith Hernandez—who tied for the honor with 216 votes apiece, even though they may not have actually tied. That year, one unknown National League writer split his 4th place vote between the Niekro brothers, Phil and Joe, each getting 3.5 points instead of the full seven points a 4th place vote was worth. But if each tied for 4th, then the 5th place finisher was really 6th and everybody after that also received one point less. If either Stargell or Hernandez was lower than 4th on that writer's ballot, then he would have lost a point from his total and the other would have won outright. Regardless, a strong case can be made the real NL MVP in 1979 was outfielder Dave Winfield, who had a monster year while playing in a pitcher-friendly park in San Diego.

Who, thus far, is the only player to win back-to-back MVP Awards with two different teams?

Barry Bonds, in 1992 with the Pirates and 1993 with the Giants after signing in San Francisco as a free agent.

What MVP winner fell short of winning the only Triple Crown by a player at his position when he failed to touch first base while attempting to beat out a ground ball on his last at-bat of the season?

Al Rosen, a runaway MVP winner in 1953, came within a whisker of edging Washington's Mickey Vernon for the AL batting title that year. The Cleveland third baseman won both the home run and RBI crowns and appeared to beat out an infield hit against Detroit's Al Aber that would have given him the batting title as well but was declared out at first by umpire Hank Soar. Photographs later validated that Rosen's final stride had been a frantic leap that landed just inches short of the bag a split second before Tigers first baseman Walt Dropo gathered in the throw from third baseman Ray Boone. The moment was riddled with irony. Rosen not only missed becoming the lone third baseman to win a Triple Crown but had lost a controversial Rookie of the Year Award to Dropo in 1950 and earlier in the 1953 season had played beside Boone in Cleveland before Boone was traded to the

Tigers, where he quickly became one of the American League's better third basemen.

In 1977, when Reds outfielder George Foster's 52 homers and .300+ batting average catapulted him to the NL MVP Award, who led the majors in OPS and won the AL MVP Award?

Rod Carew, who hit only 14 homers for the Twins but batted an AL-top .388 and racked up a 1.019 OPS. Carew won other batting titles, but 1977 rather strangely was the lone season in which he scored 100 runs or had 100 RBI.

Who won an MVP Award while playing for a team that logged a .414 winning percentage, the lowest ever by a club that featured a league MVP?

Cal Ripken in 1991 was almost the whole show for the last-place Orioles as he became only the second shortstop at that time (Ernie Banks was the first in 1958) to enjoy a season in which he batted .300 with at least 30 home runs and 100 RBI.

What first baseman won his third consecutive Gold Glove Award despite playing just 28 games in the field, a record low by a GG winner?

In 1999, Rafael Palmeiro of the Texas Rangers won both the AL Silver Slugger Award for the DH non-position and a Gold Glove for his non-work at first base. Talk about voters wearing blinders!

When the Colorado Rockies won their only pennant to date in 2007, who was their lone player to finish in the top 15 in MVP balloting?

Outfielder Matt Holliday finished 2nd in the 2007 voting to Phillies shortstop Jimmy Rollins. Many felt Holliday was penalized because his big bat was swung by a player wearing a Rockies uniform. The only other Rockies player to receive votes, shortstop Troy Tulowitzki and outfielder Brad Hawpe, finished 18th and 24th, respectively.

Who is the only World Series MVP to play for the losing team?

Second baseman Bobby Richardson of the 1960 Yankees. The Yanks outscored the Pirates 55–27 but lost the series 4 games to 3 on Bill Mazeroski's Game 7 walk-off home run. Richardson, who had 11 hits, eight runs scored, and 12 RBI over the seven games was selected as the *Sporting News* World Series MVP. Three years later, in 1964, he collected a World Series record 13 hits with a .406 average but once again in a losing cause as the Yankees fell to the Cardinals in seven games. Richardson was the original "Mr. October." In his 12 seasons—all with the Yankees—he batted .305 in fall play but just .266 in regular season action with a .299 on-base percentage.

In 1959, the top five in voting for the American League MVP Award were all members of the pennant-winning White Sox and the second-place Indians. Three of the five are in the Hall of Fame and two never will be. Name all five.

In order: Nellie Fox, Luis Aparicio, Early Wynn, Rocky Colavito, and Tito Francona. The two Indians, Colavito and Francona, remain outside the Hall. Aparicio, Wynn, and Fox are long-time residents.

The 1959 season marked only the second time since the BBWAA awards were originated in 1931 that no member of the Yankees finished in the top five in balloting. What was the first such season? The highest Yankee in the vote count that year finished 15th and led the club in triples, total bases, home runs, and RBI.

It was 1946. Charlie Keller was the top Yankees' vote getter but deserved to finish higher than 15th in his last full season. Two other Yankees, Spud Chandler and Aaron Robinson, finished in a three-way tie for 16th with Detroit's George Kell (with 12 votes each).

5***** In the 1981 strike-shortened season an outfielder compiled a .294 on-base-percentage and a .774 OPS but nonetheless finished 4th in his league in MVP balloting largely because he tied for the AL lead in homers with 22 while an infielder, who also tied for the dinger crown, led the AL in slugging and finished ten spots lower. Name both.

Outfielder Tony Armas of the A's. Meanwhile, second baseman Bobby Grich of the Orioles—who also tied for the AL lead in homers and outhit Armas in almost every other positive batting department by a comfortable margin—finished 14th in MVP voting despite topping the loop in slugging.

Hall of Fame Humdingers

Who is the only man with over 1,000 career walks but fewer than 1,500 career hits to make the Hall of Fame solely for his playing accomplishments?

Ralph Kiner, with 1,011 walks and 1,451 hits—but 369 of those hits were home runs. Miller Huggins also is in the Hall with over 1,000 walks and less than 1,500 hits but made it as a manager. Several others who made it solely for their playing accomplishments also own fewer than 1,500 hits, but only Kiner's Cooperstown credentials among the fewer than 1,500 hits brigade have never been seriously disputed.

A certain Hall of Famer's big-league debut came behind the plate at the age of nineteen. Twenty-six years later, he caught his last major-league game. His final day in the show saw him appear as a catcher in both ends of a season-ending doubleheader at Sportsmen's Park in St. Louis. He went out in a blaze of glory, homering twice in the 1st game and stealing his 277th career base in the nightcap.

The catching clue may seem misleading to some, but it really shouldn't be. Cap Anson caught over 100 games in his incredibly long 27-year playing career and was the first player in history to catch a full game, let alone a doubleheader, at age forty-five. In addition to first base, his most frequently played position, he also served as a regular at third base and in the outfield. For a variety of reasons, Anson's reputation has taken a severe hit in recent years, but no one else in the nineteenth century put together a 15-year string as good as his, from 1875–1889.

Who was the first pitcher to make the Hall of Fame after collecting more mound appearances than Cy Young collected decisions? Among his many other feats and firsts, he logged a no-hitter one season on the final day of summer in his 399th game pitched.

It was Hoyt Wilhelm who posted 52 starts, including a no-hitter on September 21, 1958, with the Orioles, among his then-record 1,070 hill appearances by the time he retired.

What Hall of Famer, at age thirty-one, hit .305 and scored a league-leading 112 runs, then quit the game after a year-long conflict with his Hall of Fame manager to tend to his California cattle ranch? After sitting out for three full seasons, he was coaxed into returning to baseball with his same team after his nemesis manager had been suspended. He was rewarded with his lone World Series ring and retired for keeps the following year with the 2nd highest career batting average among players at his primary position. Name his nemesis manager into the bargain.

Arky Vaughan, whose .318 career BA is 2nd only to Honus Wagner among shortstops eligible for the Hall of Fame. His three-year career hiatus in his prime is the longest of any Hall of Famer, save for those with an armed service(s) interruption. Vaughan clashed with Brooklyn manager Leo Durocher in 1943 after the skipper suspended pitcher Bobo Newsom for insubordination and remained out of the game until 1947 when Durocher himself was suspended for the season by Commissioner Happy Chandler for his gambling connections and was replaced at the Dodgers' helm by Burt Shotton.

Which of the following Hall of Famers was the only one to bat .300 or better in a minimum of 300 at-bats in his final season in the show? Bill Terry, Hugh Duffy, Tris Speaker, Cap Anson, Ted Williams, Billy Hamilton, George Brett, or Tony Gwynn?

Ted Williams batted .316 in 310 at-bats in 1960, his final season. Bill Terry also hit .300 in his finale but had just 229 at-bats. Before Kirby Puckett in 1995, the game had yet to see a Hall of Famer post a .300 average in his final season with enough plate appearances to qualify for the batting title. Roberto Clemente, prior to his untimely death after the 1972 season, came the closest with a .312 BA in 378 at-bats.

When Adrián Beltré makes the Hall of Fame, whose career record will he surpass for the most hits by a player who was primarily a third baseman?

George Brett, who had 3,154 hits to Beltré's 3,166.

Phil Niekro notched all but 31 of his 318 career wins after he turned thirty and 121 wins after he passed his fortieth birthday. Who remains the only pitcher in the Hall of Fame to collect all his wins in major-league garb after his thirtieth birthday?

Dazzy Vance had a 0–8 career mark when he returned to the majors to stay at age thirty-one in 1922. He posted his 197th and final career win in 1935 at age forty-four with the Brooklyn Dodgers. Vance was also the only pitcher prior to expansion in 1961 to fan 2,000 or more batters after age thirty.

In 2011, what one-time batting champ and MVP-winning shortstop became the first man to be inducted into both the college baseball and basketball Halls of Fame? He was the first-round draft pick of the NBA Fort Wayne Pistons in 1952 after setting a new NCAA record (since broken) by scoring 831 points as a guard in his junior year at Duke and was enshrined in the basketball Hall of Fame in 2006.

Dick Groat. In his 14 years as a shortstop in the majors, he played on two World Championship teams and led the NL in double plays a record five times. In his lone season in the NBA, he averaged 11.9 points a game, second on the Pistons only to center Larry Foust's 14.3. In addition to becoming the first Pirate since Paul Waner (1927) to win the NL MVP Award in 1960, he finished second in MVP balloting in 1963 after being traded— much against his will—to the Cardinals after the 1962 season.

Who was the first outfielder to make the Hall of Fame solely for his playing contributions with a sub .300 career batting average? In the year he was inducted three other position players also entered Cooperstown with sub .300 career averages. What year was it and who were the trio?

Tommy McCarthy was enshrined in 1946 along with the Cubs' immortal infield trio: Joe Tinker, Johnny Evers, and Frank Chance. McCarthy owned a .198 career batting average after his first four years of major-league play, batted .249 in his final season at age thirty-three, and left with a .292 career BA and just 1,493 hits. His entry key was serving as the other half of Boston's ballyhooed "Heavenly Twins" by playing left field beside center fielder Hugh Duffy—and at that for just four seasons (1892–1895). McCarthy is the poster boy among non-deserving Hall of Famers, but there have been less auspicious choices, including Tinker and Evers. Both, along with Chance, notched sub-.300 career BAs, but Chance arguably had the credentials to make the Hall as a manager.

Only one switch-hitter who retired prior to 1975 as a member of the 2,000-hit club has thus far failed to make the Hall of Fame. He played on flag winners, has his share of black ink, and played a position where several other Hall of Famers with far fewer offensive contributions than his have also served. Who is he?

Maury Wills, the first to steal 100 bases in a season (104 in 1962) since the present stolen base rule went into effect in 1898. In addition to his six consecutive stolen base crowns (1960–1965), he also led the National League in triples in 1962 and sacrifice hits in 1961 and was selected the NL MVP in 1962. What's more, Wills's .281 career BA leads all middle infielders and third basemen who compiled 1,500 or more hits during the era in which he played (1959–1972).

Since expansion, five lefties have won 25 or more games in a season. Each of the five had lengthy careers and also other 20-win seasons, but three are not in the Hall of Fame. All three had more career wins than one member of the pair who are in the Hall of Fame.

Does anyone really imagine Eppa Rixey was a better southpaw than Mickey Lolich, let alone Ron Guidry or Jim Kaat? All three posted more career wins than Sandy Koufax, one of the two lefty Hall of Fame 25-game winners since expansion. The other Hall of Fame southpaw pair member, Steve Carlton, is in a class by himself.

Who were the first two men voted into the Hall of Fame on the strength of their playing accomplishments even though neither ever played a single inning in the major leagues? It happened in 1972.

Negro League immortals Josh Gibson and Buck Leonard, the first two Negro League inductees.

What Hall of Famer was 2nd in home runs to Babe Ruth in the decade of 1920s (1921–1930)?

It will be surprising to some that it was not an outfielder or a first baseman. Ruth banged 462 homers during the 1920s. Second baseman Rogers Hornsby with 243 was the only one to have more than half as many homers in that decade as Ruth.

What member of the college football Hall of Fame hit a monumental walk-off pinch homer to win a World Series game?

It was the night of October 15, Game 1 of the 1988 World Series, when injury-ridden Kirk Gibson came off the Dodgers' bench to rifle a pinch homer off A's closer Dennis Eckersley. Twenty-nine years later to the night, Justin Turner slammed a walk-off three-run homer to give the Dodgers a 4–1 win over the Cubs in Game 2 of the 2017 NLCS. Gibson capped his season in 1988 with the NL MVP Award. He played only one year of college baseball while at Michigan State but helped the football Spartans tie for the Big Ten title while setting several school and Conference records as a wide receiver. Named to several All-American and Big Ten teams, Gibson was drafted by both the Detroit Tigers (in the 1st round) and the St. Louis (now Arizona) Cardinals in the 7th round of the NFL Draft. He chose baseball. Gibson later served as the manager of the Arizona Diamondbacks and is currently a color commentator for his original ML team, the Tigers.

Among all pitchers in a minimum of 1,500 innings pitched between 1920 and 1939, a 20-year stretch that heavily favored hitters, what Hall of Fame lefty topped the list in the fewest hits allowed per nine innings during that span?

Surprisingly, it was not Lefty Grove or Carl Hubbell but Lefty Gomez with 8.18 hits allowed per 9 innings. The runner-up to Gomez was Van Lingle Mungo (8.36) and tied for 3rd were Hubbell and Dazzy Vance at 8.51. Hubbell led in fewest baserunners allowed per nine innings, however, at 10.32, while Gomez ranked a mere 20th at 11.88. As for Grove, generally regarded as the premier pitcher during that period, he ranked a mere 8th in both hits and baserunners allowed per nine innings.

What Hall of Fame pitcher recorded 25 career shutouts but only 56 complete games? He was also a key component in a particularly memorable 1–0 shutout in World Series play that was also not a complete game.

Tom Glavine, the starter in Game 6 of the 1995 World Series. Sparked by David Justice's solo homer in the sixth inning, Glavine whitewashed Cleveland for eight innings before Mark Wohlers took over in the ninth frame to bring the Braves their lone World Championship under Hall of Fame manager Bobby Cox, 4 games to 2.

Who was the first future Hall of Famer since Jim Galvin (in 1875) to play in his hometown the first year it had a major-league franchise?

Born in St. Louis, Galvin debuted in 1875 with the National Association St. Louis Reds. For those who don't consider the 1875 NA a major league, Duke Snider in 1958, after the Dodgers moved from Brooklyn to Los Angeles, was the very first future Hall of Famer to play in his hometown in its maiden season as a major-league entry. The lefty slugger was born in Los Angeles in 1926 but was far from happy to be returning to his hometown in his 12th major-league season when he saw that the right field stands in the Los Angeles Coliseum, temporarily the Dodgers' new home park, were 440-feet from home plate. In the four years the Dodgers played in the Coliseum, no member of the club ever hit more than 14 home runs in a season at his home ground and only three players hit as many as 14: Charlie Neal in 1958, Frank Howard in 1960, and Wally Moon in 1959 and 1961. Moon, a left-handed hitter, tailored his swing to launch high, arcing "Moon Shots" over the towering screen barring the short access from home plate to the leftfield stands.

In his 19 major-league seasons, he became the first to catch 2,000 major-league games and the first to catch 1,000 games in both the National and American leagues. He also caught the only southpaw to win 25 or more games in a National League season since Sandy Koufax. Despite all this, he is not in the Hall of Fame. Who is he?

Bob Boone, the son of Ray Boone and father of Aaron and Bret Boone. The southpaw he caught was Steve Carlton, a 27-game winner for the last-place Phillies in 1972. Boone was a four-time All-Star, played on a World Championship team (the 1980 Phillies), and caught over 100 games in a season twice after passing the age of forty. He fanned only 608 times in 7,245 at-bats and compiled a .661 OPS—not bad for a catcher but not particularly noteworthy either. True, his .661 mark was 27 points below the position average during his time, but given his enormous longevity, steady defensive work, and several significant catching firsts, is that reason enough for him to languish outside the Hall?

What Hall of Fame slugger batted .196 and fanned 136 times in just 367 at-bats in his first full season in the majors? Sixteen years later, in his final season, he hit .203.

No, not Reggie Jackson. The answer is Mike Schmidt. Jackson gave him a run, however, hitting .178 as a partial-season rookie in 1967 (with 46 strikeouts in 118 at-bats) and .220 in his final campaign.

The first major-league player to score 1,000 career runs tallied his first run as a member of a team representing a city in Connecticut and played his last big-league game the first year the 154-game schedule was permanently adopted. Who is this Hall of Famer?

Jim O'Rourke broke in with the Middletown Mansfields of Connecticut, a short-lived National Association entry in 1872, and last appeared in the majors in 1904 at age fifty-four when he caught a full nine-inning game for the New York Giants after they had clinched their first National League pennant under John McGraw. O'Rourke spent most of his prime years in the 1880s with the Giants and played with many Hall of Famers over the course of his long career, but McGraw was not one of them, though they played against each other in 1892 and '93.

What Hall of Famer was the last player prior to Stan Musial to collect as many as 3,000 career hits?

Paul Waner, with 3,152.

The Giants' franchise is often said, wrongly, to have had a record four pitchers win their 300th games in Giants garb. All, of course, are in the Hall of Fame, but chances are you may have to mull a bit before you can name them and single out the one that won his 300th with a New York team but not the National League Giants before returning to the Giants the following year.

The four are Tim Keefe, Mickey Welch, Christy Mathewson, and Randy Johnson. Johnson's 303rd and final win came with the Giants in 2009, his only season with them. Keefe's 300th came in 1890 with the New York Players League (NYPL) entry. In 1891, after the Players League folded, he rejoined the NL Giants.

What two outfielders faced Babe Ruth in a Yankees uniform at some point during their major-league careers in postseason play and are presently in the Hall of Fame despite compiling fewer than 3,000 regular-season hits between them?

Sorry about that if your buzzer went off on Hack Wilson. Wilson was a member of both Giants and Cubs pennant winners during Ruth's major-league sojourn, but on neither occasion faced Ruth's Yankees in the Series. The two are Chick Hafey and Ross Youngs, neither of whom collected as many as 1,500 career hits.

Cap Anson played a record 27 full seasons in the majors (since tied by Nolan Ryan). Yet only six players who were teammates of Anson's are enshrined in the Hall of Fame. You need them all to consider yourself a Hall of Fame historian.

Mike Kelly, John Clarkson, Deacon White, Al Spalding, Hugh Duffy, and Clark Griffith. A seventh, Bill Dahlen, belongs in the Hall but won no popularity contests during his heyday.

The 1927 A's featured an all future Hall of Fame outfield in numerous games. Name the Hall of Fame trio, each of whom hit over .320 and played in over half the A's games.

True, the A's did feature an outfield one year of Tris Speaker, Ty Cobb, and Al Simmons at times, but that came in 1928 and Speaker did not hit .300 or play in half the team's games. A year earlier, however, the A's had Zack Wheat to combine with Cobb and Simmons and give them an outfield trio of .320+ hitters. When Connie Mack's crew broke through in 1929 to win their first pennant in 15 years, only Simmons was still with the team.

Pitchers excluded, who was the most recent player to retire with a minimum of 200 sacrifice hits and subsequently make the Hall of Fame?

Nellie Fox was the man until 2002 when Ozzie Smith got his plaque in the Hall. Fox retired in 1965 with 208 sacrifice hits; Smith in 1996 with 214. This book is made for you if your mind scrolled through people like Rizzuto and Reese before landing on Fox and then leaping ahead to Smith.

Four position players in the Hall never produced a sacrifice hit. All were right-handed hitters. Name all four and you're at the head of the class.

Jim O'Rourke is credited with zero sacrifice hits, but the bulk of his career was over before sacrifice hits were officially recorded. The quartet who all played in eras when they were scrupulously recorded are: Mike Piazza, Frank Thomas, Vladimir Guerrero, and Harmon Killebrew, the first to do it.

What Hall of Famer was the last living member of the final World Series winner managed by Miller Huggins?

Hug's last Series winner was the 1928 Yankees who swept the St. Louis Cardinals. The last surviving member of that team was catcher Bill Dickey, who died at age eighty-six in 1993. He appeared in only 10 games his frosh season, his first on August 15, 1928, at age twenty-one, but the following year became the only Yankees receiver apart from Wally Schang and Pat Collins to catch as many as 100 games in a season during Huggins's tenure as their skipper.

What Hall of Famer hit over .300 in both 1928 and 1929 but in those same two seasons lost an aggregate total of 47 games and posted a combined winning percentage of .288? His .269 career batting average leads all Hall of Famers who never played regularly at any position but pitcher.

Red Ruffing. After his first 135 decisions in the majors, all notched with abysmal Red Sox teams, he owned a .289 career winning percentage. Traded to the Yankees early in the 1930 season, he proceeded to log a .643 winning percentage for the remainder of his career. Ruffing is generally regarded as the shining example of what can happen when a pitcher with an awful team joins a great one.

Who at present are the only two Hall of Famers to play in the majors and go hitless for their entire major-league careers?

Think of a pitcher active in the majors after the DH rule was introduced but gone by the time interleague play became a regular feature. Bingo—Jack Morris. But it was not as if Morris never came to bat or got on base. He actually scored four runs as a pinch-runner and collected four hitless at-bats in National League parks in World Series action. The second man is more difficult. He fanned in his only at-bat in the majors and made the Hall of Fame strictly for his managerial work with the Dodgers. Yes: Walter Alston. If you guessed Tom Lasorda take an extra base. The ex-Dodgers' skipper collected only one hit, that during his 1956 stint with the Kansas City A's.

What Hall of Famer was the last surviving major leaguer to have played against Lou Gehrig, Lou Boudreau, Mickey Cochrane, and Mickey Mantle?

He was also the last surviving player active in the 1930s and the last living member of the 1946 Boston Red Sox. Bobby Doerr, who died in 2017.

Name the three Hall of Famers who compiled 500 or more career home runs but finished with an OPS below .850.

For shame if you guessed Harmon Killebrew because his .256 career BA is the lowest among 500-homer men. The trio, in order, is Reggie Jackson (.846), Eddie Murray (.836), and Ernie Banks (.830). Killebrew finished with a .884 OPS, not that far behind Ken Griffey Jr.'s .907.

We are now talking about two Hall of Fame pitchers. Both won over 200 games in the majors. Both were born in the same year in Midwestern states. Both spent most of their careers with the same team, yet they were never teammates. Nor did they ever play against each other or even appear in the same major or minor league at the same time. The younger of the two won his last major-league game before the older won his first. Impossible? Far from it. Who are they?

Amos Rusie was born on May 30, 1871, in Mooresville, Indiana, and made his big-league debut with the National League Indianapolis Hoosiers on May 9, 1889. In 1890, he moved to the New York Giants and last pitched for them in 1898 before engaging in a two-year holdout. His final major-league appearances came with the Cincinnati Reds in 1901. Rusie collected his last win at age twenty-seven in 1898. Joe McGinnity was born in Rock Island, Illinois, on March 19, 1871, and made his major-league debut with the National League Baltimore Orioles on April 18, 1899. More than two months older than Rusie, he bagged his first major-league win that year at age twenty-eight. In 1900, he joined Brooklyn after the Baltimore club folded but then jumped to the American League with its fledgling Baltimore entry in 1901. McGinnity joined the Giants in 1902 after Rusie had left the game and spent the remainder of his career with them.

Pete Browning owns the highest career batting average (.341) among Hall of Fame–eligible hitters not yet enshrined. Who has the second highest, at .336, with these same eligibility qualifiers for the Hall, including 10 or more seasons in the majors? He broke in as a second baseman but couldn't cut it there because of a right shoulder injury incurred during his college football days as a running back with the Crimson Tide.

Riggs Stephenson. His bum shoulder consigned him to being a weak-armed left fielder for the remainder of his career after he failed at both second and third base, and it was a relatively short career that resulted in 1,310 games and 4,508 at-bats, most of which came with the Chicago Cubs. Stephenson received a total of only eight votes in the four years he was on the Hall of Fame ballot and has never gotten any consideration from the Veterans Committee. Was he better than Chick Hafey? Lloyd Waner? Ross Youngs? Probably all three of them, but good luck taking up his cause. The same applies to Browning, whose case has best been made thus far by Philip Von Borries in *American Gladiator*, the only full-length treatment of the eccentric first hitter to popularize Louisville Slugger bats.

He led the National League in stolen bases with 26 as a rookie left fielder with the Cardinals. The following year he appeared in his first of several World Series. Prior to his death at age ninety-five he was the oldest living Hall of Famer ever to have won a stolen base crown. Among the still extant Hall of Famers, only Willie Mays would seem to be a viable candidate to one day break his record.

Red Schoendienst, who died in 2018. Red played left field only in his rookie year and never again was much of a stolen-base threat. But he is arguably among the few Hall members who could have made it either as a player or as a manager-executive.

Who are the only three members of the 500-homer club to compile as many as 100 career triples?

Willie Mays (140), Babe Ruth (135), and Jimmie Foxx (125). Congrats if you got all three of these Hall of Famers. Even many experts go for Aaron or Mantle rather than Foxx.

5***** *Who is the only position player to make the Hall of Fame solely for his playing accomplishments despite posting a career on-base percentage below .300?*

If you went for a catcher like Ray Schalk, you took a wrong path. Schalk's .340 OBP is actually the equal of Cal Ripken's and some 22 points better than Brooks Robinson's. The correct answer is Bill Mazeroski with a .299 OBP, trailing even several pitchers, including Clark Griffith. Apart from his iconic World Series–ending home run in 1960, Maz's case for belonging in the Hall rests almost entirely on his glove.

Strikeout Kings

Strikeouts were the big story in 2018 when, for the first time in major-league history, the number of strikeouts exceeded the number of hits. All of these pitchers and hitters performed strikeout feats that were significant, some positive and some negative.

After the BBWAA began bestowing awards in each league in 1931, who was the first MVP winner to top his league in batter strikeouts?

This one separates the truly great baseball historians from the near greats. Many near greats know that Joe Gordon was voted the BBWAA MVP in 1942 despite leading the AL circuit in errors at his position, grounding into double plays, and batter strikeouts are likely to assume he is the correct answer. The A-listers know that in 1933 Jimmie Foxx, in the process of winning his second consecutive MVP Award, led the AL with 93 Ks. The first MVP to lead the NL in strikeouts was Dolph Camilli of the Dodgers in 1941, when he led for his fourth and final time. Some will also know that in 1930, the season before BBWAA awards began officially awarded in both leagues annually, Hack Wilson, the league MVP, paced the NL in strikeouts. Although Foxx is the correct answer, Wilson is certainly arguably correct as well in that the voting in 1930 was done by the BBWAA.

What pitcher will never make the Hall of Fame even though he compiled the most strikeouts in a season during the 1980s?

Valenzuela is not a bad guess, but it was Mike Scott of the Astros with 306 Ks in 1986. It was a year out of nowhere. Even though Scott toiled nearly 2,000 innings in the 1980s, he ranks only 7th in total Ks that decade and is just 14th in Ks per nine innings pitched with 6.51.

What pre-expansion era Hall of Famer held the season record for the most strikeouts by a batter under the age of twenty before yielding this dubious distinction to a post-expansion Hall of Famer?

Mickey Mantle, with 74 in 1951. The record, believe it or not, was held for 19 years by a pitcher: John "Egyptian" Healy, with 67 in 1886. The current mark belongs to Bryce Harper, who had 120 in 2012. Mantle's successor, Ken Griffey Jr., was the post-expansion record holder prior to Harper with 83.

At the close of the nineteenth century, who was the only pitcher to date that had registered as many as 2,000 strikeouts?

Tim Keefe, with 2,564. Second to Keefe with 1,978 was John Clarkson. Amos Rusie, probably the hardest thrower prior to

Walter Johnson, was third with 1,944. Matt Kilroy, who had set the season record of 513 Ks in 1886, ranked only 22nd on the list after overuse shortened his career.

What hurler in his first year as an ERA qualifier gave up 208 walks, allowed 14.24 baserunners per nine innings, and was unable to vote that year on Election Day but posted a .607 winning percentage (17–11) for a non-pennant winner largely on the strength of his 240 strikeouts?

Bob Feller was nineteen years of age in 1938 when he tied the then all-time single-game record by fanning 18 Detroit Tigers in a losing effort.

Who is the only catcher to top his league in batter strikeouts since 1893, when the current pitching distance was set? He was twenty-four at the time and fanned 77 times in 398 at-bats. That same year he set a new single-season record for the most home runs by a catcher that he broke five years later (but no longer holds).

The year was 1925, and the catcher was Gabby Hartnett. His 24 homers broke Jack Clements's catchers' mark of 17, set in 1893. Hartnett crushed 37 home runs in 1930 with just 62 strikeouts to set a season standard for backstops that lasted until 1953, when Roy Campanella banged 41 dingers. The current career record holder is Mike Piazza with 396.

Pittsburgh joined the National League in 1887 after a five-year stint in the rebel American Association. In 1891, right-hander Mark Baldwin set a new Pittsburgh NL franchise record when he fanned 197 hitters. His record stood for over 70 years. Who finally broke it?

Bob Veale, with 250 Ks in 1964. The following year he upped the mark to 276, which still stands as the all-time Pirates record. Indeed, he is the only Pirates hurler to log multiple 200+ strike-out seasons—four in all.

Among retired players who spent the vast majority of their careers at shortstop, who presently holds the record for the most career Ks by a shortstop?

Derek Jeter, with 1,840 career whiffs, topping even free-swingers like Dave Kingman. Jeter had nine seasons in which he fanned 100 or more times and three in which he fanned 99 times. He also whiffed 135 times in 650 at-bats in the postseason. None of this should be terribly surprising considering his longevity, but it still should be of interest to historians that the record prior to expansion in 1961 belonged to Pee Wee Reese with 890, less than half Jeter's total.

Who is the only pitcher between 1901 and the emergence of Sandy Koufax to post back-to-back seasons in which he fanned 300 or more hitters?

This one is harder than it looks. Walter Johnson never did it, nor did Feller. It was Rube Waddell in 1903 and 1904. His 302 Ks in 1903 are particularly impressive because it was the last season the schedule still called for only 140 games.

When Brad Eldred of the Pirates fanned 77 times in 190 at-bats in 2005, whose long-standing season record did he break for the most batter strikeouts in less than 200 at-bats? The free swinger in question still holds several contact futility records. Meanwhile, Eldred's record lasted just 11 years before it was shattered by Alex Avila of the White Sox with 78 Ks in just 169 at-bats in 2016.

In 1962, Dave Nicholson of the Orioles fanned 76 times in 173 at-bats. (Note that Nicholson's record of 76 was tied in 2000 by Russell Branyan of the Indians.) For years, Nicholson also held the record for the most Ks in a season with 175 in 1963. Among players with a minimum of 1,000 career at-bats, his 573 Ks in 1,419 at-bats for a .404 whiff rate per at-bat is still the all-time high. On May 6, 1964, Nicholson, by then with the White Sox, in the first game of a doubleheader against Kansas City, walloped a home run in Comiskey Park that some authorities believe was the longest four-bagger in big-league history. There were other momentous moments like it in his career but too few in all to convince any team that his long balls would ever outweigh his gargantuan strikeout totals.

What slugger in recent memory spent 14 seasons in the majors, compiled 194 home runs to go with just 467 RBI and in 2,934 at-bats gave Nicholson a hard run for his money when he finished with a .381 whiff rate per at-bat? His .814 career OPS kept buyers in the market for his left-handed swing until 2011, when he was well past his 35th birthday.

Russell Branyan again. In 2002, he fanned 151 times in 378 at-bats, only the third hitter to top 150 Ks in fewer than 400 at-bats. Preceding him were Bo Jackson in 1987 and Melvin Nieves in 1997. Since then, eight players have accomplished such a feat, with two doing so in 2018 alone (Mike Zunino of the Mariners, 150 Ks in 373 at-bats; and Ian Happ of the Cubs, 167 Ks with 387 at-bats).

Name the only National League hurler in the decade of the 1940s to fan as many as 200 batters in a season.

Johnny Vander Meer of the Reds, with 202 in 1941.

Who was the last player to lead either the American or National League in batter strikeouts with a total of less than 100?

Phillies outfielder Harry Anderson, with 95 in 1958. He nonetheless succeeded in batting .301 with a .897 OPS, both career highs.

Hack Wilson at one time held the National League—record for the most seasons leading the league in strikeouts with five. It was a short-lived record. Who broke Wilson's record less than 15 years after he set it by fanning 91 times for the Phillies in 1945, his last full major-league season?

The eldest of the three DiMaggio brothers, Vince. In 1938, Vince fanned 134 times to set a new NL season record that lasted until 1960 when it was broken by Phillies first baseman Pancho Herrera with 136 whiffs. Vince still holds the NL record for the most seasons as the strikeout leader with six, the last four in succession—1942–1945.

What Blue Jays pitcher set an all-time season record in 1987 when he fanned 128 batters but failed to win a game, finishing 0–6?

The answer is obviously a reliever, but you probably have to know your Blue Jays to recall that it was Tom Henke, their closer that year with a league-leading 34 saves and a 2.49 ERA. It was not the only year Henke went winless as the Jay's closer. In 1991, he finished 0–2 with 32 saves.

Who was the first position player to have the dubious distinction of winning the batting whiff title in both leagues?

Jim Thome led the AL in batter Ks with the Indians in 1999 and again in 2001. After leaving Cleveland as a free agent to join the Phillies, he topped the NL with 182 Ks in 2003.

Among retired pitchers with over 2,000 career strikeouts who holds the record for the fewest wins?

Prior to 2013, it belonged to Sam McDowell, who fanned 2,453 batters in 2,492 innings with 141 wins. He also had a stellar 3.17 career ERA but was plagued by wildness and seldom pitching for decent teams. The record is now owned by Ryan Dempster, who finished his career in 2013 with 132 wins and 2,075 Ks.

What slugger in his first season as a starter led the AL in Ks in 2007, even though he had less than 400 at-bats?

Jack Cust of the Oakland A's. In 2007, he also spent part of the season with Portland in the Pacific Coast League. Cust won three AL whiff crowns with the A's even though he had only three seasons in which he was a batting title qualifier.

Until quite recently it was believed that the first batter to fan more than 100 times in an American League season was Danny Moeller of the Washington Senators in 1912. But lately there has been a flurry of excellent research into batter strike-outs in seasons where totals were previously unknown. Now the first batter to fan more than 100 times in an American League season is established to have been another Danny, an outfielder with the pennant-winning Athletics in 1905. What is Danny's last name?

Hoffman, with 105 Ks in 1905. He also fanned 103 times with the New York Yankees in 1907. His poor contact remains a bit of mystery. In his career he produced only a .328 slugging average in nine seasons and never had more than 21 extra-base hits in a season. But the likely explanation for the holes in his swing is a near-fatal beanball he suffered at the hand of Red Sox lefty Jesse Tannehill on July 1, 1904. Hoffman, a left-handed hitter, was forever afterward easy prey for left-handed curveballs and was often platooned.

In the decade of the 1930s, who was the lone National League hurler to whiff 200 or more batters in a season? He did it in the only year he topped the NL in pitcher Ks.

Brooklyn Dodgers right-hander Van Lingle Mungo fanned 238 hitters in 1938, a remarkable achievement in that no NL hurler between 1925 and 1958 whiffed more.

When Dodgers southpaw Sandy Koufax fanned 382 batters in 1965, whose all-time National League record did he only moderately threaten? Extra credit if you know the rule change in the NL prior to the season in which the record was set that produced higher strikeout totals across the board.

Koufax fell 59 Ks short of Charley Radbourn's NL record 441 Ks for the Providence Grays in 1884 when he won 59 games, also a record. Higher strikeout totals in the 1884 NL were enabled by the rule that legalized overhand pitching for the first time that season. Oddly enough, Radbourn did not benefit much from the rule change as he threw mostly sidearm.

What hurler's 3,574 career Ks are the most by a pitcher who was never a strikeout leader in either the NL or the AL? Hint: He pitched in both.

Don Sutton, whose personal high in 23 major-league seasons was 217 with the Dodgers in 1969.

Subsequent to the 1981 season when only a partial schedule was played owing to a prolonged player strike and no hurlers registered as many as 200 Ks, what was the most recent season that a pitching strikeout leader notched fewer than 200 Ks?

Len Barker of the Indians led the AL in Ks with just 127 in the strike-shortened 1981 season. Barker also led the year before with 187, when a full schedule was played. Much of the reason for Barker's twin triumphs was that Nolan Ryan skipped to the NL prior to the 1980 season after topping the AL in Ks in seven of the previous eight years. Since Barker's back-to-back K leading seasons, the only leader with fewer than 200 Ks was Andy Benes, who topped the NL with 189 in 1994, but that too was a drastically strike-shortened season. The lowest total by a full-season leader since 1981 belongs to Jose DeLeon of the Cardinals with 201 in 1989.

In the first expansion season, what rookie set a new American League K record when he fanned 141 times in his only year as a qualifier? Hint: He was a second baseman.

The year of course was 1961, and the rookie second baseman was Jake Wood of the Tigers. Despite his high K total, he was viewed as a very promising prospect, swiping 30 bases in 39 attempts and leading the AL in triples with 14. But he never developed.

In his 13 and a fraction seasons in the majors (1920–1933), Joe Sewell fanned only 114 times in regular-season action in 7,132 at-bats. Among players with a minimum of 5,000 career at-bats during that same time, who had the second-fewest Ks?

Sam Rice, with 185 Ks in 7,563 at-bats. No one else with as many as 5,000 at-bats in that same span fanned less than 200 times. Rice in addition compiled a .322 career BA. It doesn't take much work to build a case that Rice is among the most underrated players in history. Spending the first 19 seasons of his 20-year career in Washington with the Senators hurt him immeasurably but perhaps no more than his small size and failure to draw many walks.

What first baseman is the only player who debuted after 1919 to fan less than 200 times in a minimum of 5,000 career at-bats, yet failed to compile a .300 career batting average? The only clue you should need is he won an MVP Award.

Frank McCormick, the 1940 NL MVP, whiffed 189 times in 5,723 at-bats and finished with a .299 career BA.

Jim Galvin, the first 300-game winner in major-league history, holds the record for the most career batter Ks by a pitcher with 631, not including two seasons where his K totals as a hitter are still unavailable. What fellow 300-game winner is second only to Galvin in batter Ks by a pitcher with 593? Hint: He posted a .148 career batting average in 17 seasons and was a league leader in pitching Ks his rookie year with a total of just 116.

Lefty Grove, who began his major-league career with the A's by leading the AL in Ks in each of his first seven seasons. A 300-game winner who was a league strikeout leader as a rookie should have been a huge clue.

Among all catchers with a minimum of 5,000 at-bats, who has the highest on-base percentage, the highest batting average, and the fewest strikeouts?

None other than Grove's long-time battery mate, Mickey Cochrane.

What Hall of Famer is the only player since the present pitching distance was set in 1893 to play in at least half his team's games, compile a minimum of 200 at-bats, and not strike out all season? In over 7,700 career at-bats, he whiffed only 173 times, yet he had nearly as many negative offensive features as positive ones, including only 430 career walks.

Lloyd Waner in 1941 split the season between the Pirates and the Braves and made contact in every one of his 219 at-bats but tallied only 26 runs.

Once career walks are deducted from career strikeouts, the owner of the highest total, to no one's surprise, is Ted Williams with 1,312 (2,021 walks—709 whiffs). Third is Barry Bonds with 1,019 (2,558 walks—1,538 Ks). Who is second with a total of 1,032?

This one will be a surprise to many readers. The answer is Eddie Collins (1,499 walks—467 Ks—1,032).

Among active players with a minimum of 1,000 walks, who is the only hitter that began the 2018 season with more career walks than Ks?

Albert Pujols with 1,251 walks and 1,146 whiffs. His plus total of 105 by the end of the 2018 season was reduced to 68 (1,279 walks and 1,211 whiffs).

Prior to expansion in 1961, who among retired players had the most career pitching strikeouts of any hurler not in the Hall of Fame?

Bobo Newsom, with 2,082. Second to Newsom was Tony Mullane, with 1,803. Five stars if you got Newsom.

What pitcher in a seven-year career started 127 games, allowed only 6.4 hits per nine innings, and fanned more batters in his first two seasons (508) than he did in his last five (329)?

If you've surmised that something bad happened after his first two seasons, you're right. The answer is Herb Score, who was forced to change his delivery after he was felled by Gil McDougald's line drive in the spring of 1957 and was unable to make an adjustment.

Who is currently the only pitcher not in the Hall of Fame despite fanning 300 or more hitters three times in his career?

Ed Morris is a terrific guess, but in his 3rd most prolific K season, he fanned only 298 batters. Sam McDowell and J. R. Richard are also good guesses, but each only had two 300-K seasons. The correct answer is Curt Schilling, whose incendiary stances on social issues since leaving the game may thus far be the only blemish keeping him out of the Hall.

5***** No one can even begin to predict how many of today's players will leave the majors with fewer than 50 career home runs and more than 1,000 career strikeouts, but at the close of the 2015 season there was only one. He bowed out with 1,144 Ks and just 41 four-baggers to go with his 2,207 hits and .285 career batting average. At that point, it was hard to imagine anyone ever again posting a similar career profile, but before leaving the majors in 2016, presumably for good, Michael Bourn collected just 36 home runs to go with 1,124 whiffs. Who was Bourn's lone predecessor?

Switch-hitter Willie Wilson. In 1988, the lone 100-K season in his 19-year career, he fanned 106 times and hit just one home run.

The Unappreciated, the Unsung, and the Unrecognized

Who were the only two players to compile as many as 1,000 hits in National League play between 1899 and 1915 and post a batting average of .330 or better?

Honus Wagner, the leader to be sure with a .333 BA. But Mike Donlin was only one point behind him at .332. Jake Beckley is 3rd on the list, but his .312 mark trails the two leaders by far.

Who is the only Japanese-born major leaguer to date to be eligible for the Hall of Fame both as a player and a manager?

Dave Roberts, born in Naha, Okinawa, Japan, was active in the majors for 10 seasons and is now managing the Dodgers. Since there is no rule on how long a manager must be at the helm of a major-league team or teams, Roberts is already eligible for the Hall as both a player and a manager.

Shohei Ohtani, the Angels' new double-duty sensation, may one day do it. But, in the meantime, who is the last major leaguer to date to collect 100 or more hits and hurl as many as 162 innings in the same season?

The knee-jerk answer is of course Babe Ruth. But it's wrong, largely because the 1918 season, when he fully began the conversion from pitcher to everyday player, was shortened by World War I, denying him the opportunity for 100 hits. Those who don't know that also may not know that the next most likely candidate, Cy Seymour, also fell short of 100 hits in any of the seasons he was primarily a pitcher. However, Seymour compiled 82 hits in 1898, and the final clues are that the correct answer is a man who did it a year earlier in 1897, played almost his entire career in the Windy City, and left the White Sox abruptly after the 1905 season to form his own semipro team in Chicago, the Logan Squares, thereupon missing out on participating in the 1906 World Series. Jimmy Callahan, erroneously known in some reference books as Nixey Callahan. In 1897, Callahan rapped 105 hits in 360 at-bats and was 12–9 on the mound with 21 complete games in 189⅔ innings.

What player ranked 4th all-time in career walks behind only Hall of Famers Babe Ruth, Ted Williams, and Mel Ott when he left the majors in 1962 (the same year that Edward Emil Kranepool debuted with the Mets) and has yet to make the Hall of Fame?

Edward Frederick Joseph Yost, who, as a Mets coach for many years, shared the same locker room with Kranepool. Yost collected 1,863 career hits and 1,614 walks, including a high of 151 in 1956 when he garnered just 119 hits.

What player at the close of a certain season owned the top batting average in the majors among qualifiers but failed to win the batting crown in either league?

In 1990, outfielder Willie McGee of the Cardinals, the 1985 National League batting leader, was in a contract year. Since he was likely to demand more than the Cards felt he was worth, they dealt him just before the trade deadline to Oakland for three prospects. Upon leaving the NL, McGee's stats froze. He was hitting .335 at the time with enough plate appearances to qualify for the batting title and was second in the NL in hitting to Lenny Dykstra's .340 mark. With the A's, McGee hit just .274 in 29 games, reducing his composite average to .324. But his frozen .335 NL BA proved good enough to stay at the top when Dykstra slipped to .325. Meanwhile, Eddie Murray of the Dodgers came on strong in the last month of the season and finished at .330, one point ahead of George Brett, the American League leader at .329. Even though McGee's composite figure of .324 was only the 6th best in the majors, he earned his second NL batting crown while Murray, with the best full-season BA in the majors, came up empty.

The most recent player to compile 3,000 hits and never serve as a DH was gone from the scene by the time the DH rule came into existence. Who is he?

Roberto Clemente, who collected his 3,000th hit in his final major-league plate appearance in 1972. That winter he lost his life in a plane crash just weeks before the DH rule was first implemented in the AL. Clemente was flirting with retirement at the time and would almost certainly have done so had he lived and the Pirates had dealt him to an American League team, where he might have been employed as a DH.

Bert Campaneris holds the record for the most games played in an A's uniform (1,795), but he also played with three other teams. Who holds the record for the most games played solely in an A's uniform and no other with 1,421? While a member of the Athletics, he made his summer home in two different cities.

Pete Suder, also the A's all-time leader into grounding into double plays with 158. Somewhat ironically, he was the primary second baseman on the 1949 club that set a team record of 217 double plays, which stood until 2010. Suder finished his career in 1955, the year the A's franchise moved to Kansas City. He was among the last surviving A's who had played under Connie Mack when he died in 2006 at the age of ninety.

After Frank Selee left the Boston National League franchise and assumed the reins of the Chicago Cubs following the 1901 season, who was the franchise's only manager to finish with a winning record in every full season he skippered the Boston club before it moved to Milwaukee in 1953?

Hope you didn't make this one harder than it is. Post-Selee, the Braves had only one protracted stretch when they were contenders before leaving Boston, and that came just before they deserted Beantown. The club hired Billy Southworth prior to the 1946 season after he had narrowly missed winning a fourth-straight pennant with the Cardinals in 1945. He brought the Braves' brass three straight winning seasons, including their second and last post-1900 pennant in 1948, and also a partial winning season in 1949 (55–54) before leaving the club for health reasons and turning it over to coach Johnny Cooney. Southworth returned to the dugout in 1950 and again finished above .500. But in 1951, when the Braves were 28–31 on June 19, he asked to be allowed to resign, and the reins were given to the club's longtime star right fielder, Tommy Holmes.

Who is the only hurler on the lengthy list of career 200-game winners to work enough innings to qualify for his league's ERA crown in every season of his career? You needn't shoot yourself if you don't get the lone pitcher in history to be a qualifier in every season of his 15-year career. It's much more difficult than it may seem at first glance.

In 1931, rookie Paul Derringer finished 18–8 with the Cardinals and appeared in the World Series against the A's. Fifteen years later, in 1945, his finale, he again appeared in the World Series after going 16–11 with the Cubs. In every season of his 15-year career Derringer worked at least 174 innings and twice labored over 300 innings. He never won an ERA crown, but in 1933, after the Cards traded him to the lowly Reds, he became the last major-league hurler to lose as many as 27 games in a season. Derringer was so stingy at issuing free passes that he was called "The Control King," but away from the mound, he was anything but in control of himself. He fought with fellow players like Dizzy Dean and once threw a bottle of ink that narrowly missed owner Larry MacPhail's head.

He won a league home run crown, holds the season record for the most assists at his position, also had another season playing there where he tied for the second most assists ever at his position, and is second only to a Hall of Fame contemporary in career assists at his position. He played on four pennant winners, played in all or part of 22 seasons, compiled 390 home runs and over 2,000 hits, made the All-Star team at age forty in his second season with his hometown Padres, and has never had so much as a whiff of Hall of Fame heights. It will annoy you to no end if you don't get this one.

Graig Nettles. If you saw both him and Brooks Robinson, his Hall of Fame contemporary, in their primes, who would you rather have had at third base? Tough choice, right?

Including the nineteenth century, who is the only man, eligible for the Hall of Fame for his playing accomplishments alone, to steer his team to a World Series victory as a full-time regular player and manager and not make the Hall of Fame?

In 1891, Arthur Irwin piloted the flag-winning Boston Reds of the American Association—probably the best team in baseball that year—but was denied a World Series shot when Chicago player-manager Cap Anson had agreed to a postseason clash (which had been an annual event between the rival major league since 1884) if both his team and the Reds won. But Chicago was robbed of the National League pennant, arguably for agreeing to play the AA winner while the two leagues were at loggerheads, a story worth a book in itself. In any case, Irwin was far from being a full-time player, appearing in only six games. Bill Carrigan won the 1915 and 1916 World Series as the Red Sox' player-manager but was only a backup catcher in both seasons. Charlie Grimm won a pennant but never a World Series as a full-time player-manager with the Cubs. Lou Boudreau was the last full-time regular player to steer his club to a World Series triumph when his MVP season brought the Indians their last title to date in 1948. But Boudreau is in the Hall of Fame, as are all but one of the numerous other player-managers to match his feat. The only one who is not is Fielder Jones, the pilot and center fielder of the "Hitless Wonders," the 1906 World Champion White Sox. Jones also nearly steered the St. Louis Terriers to the 1915 Federal League pennant while playing in seven games.

Who was the last pitcher to serve as a player manager for a full season?

Clark Griffith remains the lone hurler-manager whose arm helped his fledgling American League club, the 1901 Chicago White Sox, bag a pennant—and that includes the nineteenth century. The last pitcher to run a major-league club for a full season was Fred Hutchinson of the 1953 Tigers. Hutchinson, who was nearing the end of a long pitching career with the Tigers, was handed the Detroit reins the previous year after Red Rolfe was fired. He remained on the roster all of 1952 and again in 1953, his first full year as a helmsman, but appeared in only three games, all in relief. Eight years later, now strictly a bench manager, Hutchinson guided Cincinnati to a surprise pennant before losing to the Yankees in the 1961 World Series. He was still at the Reds' helm in 1964 when he was forced to turn the reins over to coach Dick Sisler shortly before succumbing to a long battle with lung cancer.

In his last start of the 2018 season, what pitcher (whose streak is still active) set a new all-time record for the most consecutive starts in which he allowed three runs or fewer?

Jacob deGrom, with the New York Mets.

The only man to play over 2,000 major-league games (2,016) and tabulate fewer than 1,500 career hits (1,316) played in four World Series. No, this isn't someone from the Deadball Era. Indeed, many of you out there saw him play. Who is he?

In 1969, his second season as the Orioles' regular shortstop, Mark Belanger hit .287 and collected 152 hits. He had only two other seasons in his 18-year career when he registered more than 111 hits (1971 and 1976), yet he was seldom in danger of losing his job. The reason is he won eight Gold Gloves, and his total zone rating is the highest ever among shortstops and the 3rd best in history at any position. Belanger is the only player in major-league history to post more than 40 Wins Above Replacement (rWAR) while logging an OPS+ under 80. What's more, his OPS+ is under 70—a rousing 68 according to Baseball-Reference's Play Index.

Who was the first player to win a major award despite not coming to bat all season?

In 1973, the first season the DH rule was in effect in the American League, the Orioles' Jim Palmer won the American League Cy Young Award. There have been numerous other such AL Cy Young winners since.

Hats off if you know the Cy Young recipient who collected the most at-bats of any winner in his award-winning season, which happened to be his final campaign.

Sandy Koufax, with 118 at-bats in 1966, his final season, when he hit a sizzling .076 to shave his career batting average to below .100 (.097). In the years since, both Fergie Jenkins in 1971 and Gaylord Perry in 1972 have won Cy Youngs with more plate appearances (132 apiece) than Koufax's 124 in 1966, but not more at-bats.

Hack Wilson holds the season RBI record with 191 in 1930 but drove home just 135 Cubs teammates that season because he also amassed a then National League record 56 home runs. Who has the season record for driving home the most teammates?

Many researchers consider Hank Greenberg's 143 teammates driven home in 1937 when he bagged 183 RBI and 40 home runs for the Tigers to be the current record, but those who believe nineteenth century RBI totals are accurate accord the honor to Sam Thompson of the 1887 Detroit Wolverines who drove home 166 runs to go with his 10 home runs, giving him 156 teammates driven home. While it's true that nineteenth-century stats are often viewed with suspicion, one must remember that Wilson's record RBI total stood for many years at 190 and only in recent years was it discovered that Jim Gentile tied Roger Maris for the American League RBI crown in 1961.

The only outfielder to total as many as 1,500 putouts in a three-year span logged exactly 1,500 but is best known for an assist that saved his first-place team from tying for the pennant on the final day of the regular season.

Just that one clue should be enough to steer most historians to Richie Ashburn, whose throw from center field on Duke Snider's one-hop single nailed Cal Abrams at the plate in the bottom of the ninth inning on the final day of the 1950 National League season to prevent the Dodgers from ending the regular campaign in a flat-out tie with Ashburn's Phillies. His 1,500 putout span was from 1956–1958.

The name of the pitcher who went 19–8 for the American League runner-up in 2007 and received mention that year in both BBWAA MVP and Cy Young balloting is no longer to be found on either list today. How can that be?

Roberto Hernandez played under the name Fausto Carmona until the 2011 season when it emerged he had come to the USA under a visa issued in a fictitious name that shaved three years off his age. He got a valid visa in 2012 under his true name after being suspended for identity fraud and then pitched under his real name from 2012 to 2016. A minor-league sensation in the Cleveland farm system in 2003 at 17–4, Hernandez/Carmona was slated to be a spot starter and mop-up reliever in 2007 after a 1–10 rookie year ledger in 2006 but became a starter after Cliff

Lee pulled an abdominal muscle and nearly pitched the Tribe to the American League flag.

Who was the only pitcher to throw the final pitch of the season one year in both Fenway Park and Braves Field?

He was also the only pitcher to clinch the pennant with a complete-game win on the final day of the regular season and earn a World Series–ending save that same year in the same city. A few moments of thought should yield the year, 1948, and the name, Gene Bearden, arguably the game's most memorable One-Year Wonder. Bearden played with 2-by-3-inch aluminum plates in his knee and head from wounds suffered in World War II when his ship was torpedoed, and he floated with comrades on a rubber raft in the boiling Pacific sun for three days before he was rescued. Fair warning: You may meet Bearden and his 1948 season again in these pages.

Many top-notch players, for a variety of reasons, did not have their careers interrupted by military service in World War II. Among those that remained active during the war years (considered to be 1942–1945), who collected the most hits? Exempted from the military because of a severe sinus condition, he originally signed with the Yankees and was on one pennant winner, but it did not come until after the war had ended and with the team that traded first baseman Buddy Hassett to the Yankees for him.

Tommy Holmes, with 744 hits. Soon after joining the Boston Braves and sewing up their right field post, he grew to be such an enormous fan favorite that the right field seats, which were rows of otherwise nondescript flat benches that sold for a buck and had been dubbed "The Jury Box" back in 1918 when a sportswriter counted only 12 fans sitting in them, became the most popular ticket in Braves Field. In 1945, along with topping the National League in home runs with a somewhat modest total of 28, Holmes hit safely in a then post-1900 National League record 37 straight games and had arguably the best season by a Boston NL hitter since Hugh Duffy in 1894. After the war, he remained a steady force in the Braves' lineup but never again approached his 1945 heights.

Once free agency came to fruition in 1975, player movement accelerated by leaps and bounds. Within a few years, a certain player began to assemble the following portfolio over a single decade. He hit .339 in 100 games as a rookie with the 1980 Phillies. He then led the National League in runs with the 1982 Cardinals. Three years later he played on the 1985 World Series winner and four years after that led the National League in OBP while a member of the 1989 Braves. All of this in the space of just 10 seasons, and yet I'll wager you've forgotten him.

Lonnie Smith. If you didn't remember him based on the clues you were given about his positive feats, would it have helped if I'd added that his baserunning gaffe in the eighth inning of Game 7 arguably decided the winner of the 1991 World Series?

The only pitcher to be on the mound for the final out of a World Series Game 7 multiple times was also one half of the last pair of starters to both pitch complete games in the seventh game of a World Series. Who is he?

Cardinals ace Bob Gibson threw the final pitches in Game 7 of both the 1964 and 1967 World Series, as St. Louis took the measure of the Yankees and the Red Sox, respectively. At the close of the sixth inning in Game 7 of the 1968 World Series, Gibson was locked in a scoreless struggle with Detroit's Mickey Lolich. A misjudged fly ball by center fielder Curt Flood resulted in the Tigers scoring three runs in the seventh frame and then cruising to a 4–1 win. Gibson nonetheless finished the game, as did Lolich. It was the last time both starters went the distance in Game 7 of a Series.

What post-World War II and pre-division play hurler finished his career with a 128–116 record? Nothing terribly remarkable about that. But he was a dazzling 28–13 in 56 appearances against the Yankees, including 49 starts, and a mediocre 100–103 against the rest of the competition.

Frank Lary, appropriately known as "The Yankee Killer."

Who were the only two brothers to date to finish first and second in a league batting race? The only clue you should need is a third brother hit .259 that year.

The season was 1966 when Matty Alou of the Pirates won the NL batting crown at .342 and brother Felipe of the Braves batted .327 for the Braves. The three Alou brothers—Matty, Felipe, and Jesus—three years earlier had formed the first all-brother outfield in the majors for the Giants. The first all-brother outfield in professional ball was formed by the Mansell brothers—Tom, Mike and John—in 1881 with the Washington C.C./Albany,

New York, minor-league club. All three later played in the majors at the same time but never with the same team.

As of 2019, Albert Pujols's production had declined sharply in every major offensive department except one since he turned thirty. What is the only offensive department where he has yet to set a new career negative since 2010?

Batter strikeouts. Pujols through 2018 had yet to fan as many as 100 times in a season. In 2017, he tied his rookie figure of 93. In almost every other offensive aspect of his game, he gave the Angels little reason not to regret he was under contract through 2020.

When Starlin Castro made his big-league debut at shortstop with the Cubs on May 7, 2010, he not only homered in his first at-bat but also drove in a debut-game-record six runs. What other first did Castro accomplish on his debut day?

He was the first major leaguer born as late as 1990 to appear in the majors. He was not, however, the first player born in the decade of the 1990s (1991–2000) to do so. The first was pitcher Julio Teheran, born on January 27, 1991, who debuted on May 7, 2011, with the Braves. Mike Trout and Jacob Turner also debuted in 2011 and were born in 1991, but their debut dates were later than Teheran's.

Who is the only Hall of Famer to date who made his final major-league appearance as a player on the Opening Day of a season as a pinch-runner for a fellow Hall of Famer? He did not make the Hall for his playing accomplishments after batting a career .199 in 132 games, most of them with a team he later managed to several postseason appearances.

On April 6, 1973, Tony La Russa made his final appearance in the bigs as a player when he entered the game as a pinch-runner for Ron Santo of the Chicago Cubs in the bottom of the ninth inning and eventually scored the game-winning run. Most of La Russa's games came with the A's, the team he managed the longest.

Twelve years after setting a positive single-season pitching record that will last forever, this player returned to the majors after a four-year absence as the Opening Day right fielder with a team that had won the National League pennant the year he set his unbreakable pitching record. Who is it?

Matt Kilroy. In 1886, as a rookie with Baltimore of the American Association, he fanned 513 hitters, but his arm strength began to desert him soon thereafter. A dozen years later, Kilroy opened the 1898 season in right field for Chicago, the 1886 NL flag winner, but eventually returned to the mound when he failed to hit consistently.

Who is the only pitcher to register a complete-game win in the final contest in two consecutive World Series and then be the losing pitcher in the Series finale the following year?

Art Nehf cemented the Giants' World Series triumphs over the Yankees in 1921 and 1922 and then dropped the game in 1923 that clinched the Yankees' first ever World Championship.

Counting only what are now considered to be official rookie seasons, whose record of 456 walks in his first four full seasons (1890–1893) did Ted Williams break in 1942 when he finished his fourth full major-league season with 495 career walks?

Jack Crooks. He walked 10 times in 12 games with the 1889 Columbus Buckeyes of the American Association after joining the team in late September, and then ran off 456 more walks in his first four full seasons, 1890–1893, including his official rookie year of 1890. Only one of those seasons came on a 154-game schedule—1892—and that year he appeared in only 128 games. Crooks's career was one of a kind. He compiled only 671 career hits but tallied 537 runs, almost all of it while playing with weak teams.

Who is the only batsman since expansion in 1961 to play in all his team's 162 games and average less than one total base per game? His batting average for the year in question was .216, and he played second base.

In 1964, Bobby Knoop of the Los Angeles Angels batted .216 with 105 hits and only 136 total bases. A rookie at the time, Knoop went on to play nine seasons in the majors and finish with a .236 batting average and a .630 OPS. He was also the first middle infielder to fan 100 or more times in each of his first five seasons. All of which made him a dismal offensive performer, right? Not really. In actuality, his career stats were just a few points shy of the major-league average (.244 BA/.643 OPS) at second base during that span (1964–1972), considered by some historians to be the second coming of the Deadball Era, with the most significant difference being that home runs were much more prevalent than triples.

5***** *Twenty-game losers are nearly extinct and may soon be so forever. Pitchers who now even approach 20 losses usually carry atrocious ERAs and seldom finish the season in the rotation. Witness Mike Maroth, the last 20-game loser to date with 21 in 2003, who clocked in with a 5.35 ERA. We'll bet plenty you don't know who was the last major-league hurler to lose 20 games despite posting a sub 3.00 ERA.*

We say last with utter confidence because Brian Kingman in 1980 (the last 20-game loser prior to Maroth) was also the last 20-game loser with a sub *4.00* ERA (3.80). The last to do it with a sub 3.00 ERA was Nate Andrews in 1943, who went 14–20 for the Boston Braves with a remarkable 2.57 ERA in what was his official rookie year. Turk Farrell gave it a good run, though, for the expansion Houston Colt 45s in 1962, finishing with a stellar 3.02 ERA despite winning just 10 of 30 decisions.

Singular Pitching Feats

Prior to expansion in 1961, Bob Grim held the record for the fewest complete games by a 20-game winner with eight in 1954. Who was the first 20-game winner to fail to complete a single game in his 20-win season? He is not in the Hall of Fame although he had numerous other 20-win seasons.

Roger Clemens in 2001 went 20–3 in 33 starts for the Yankees without completing a game. The first hurler to match Clemens's feat was also a Yankee: Mike Mussina, who went 20–9 in 34 starts during his final season of 2008. It's been done several times since.

The American League record holder for most wins in a season in which he surrendered no home runs is not in the Hall of Fame. Nor is anyone mounting a case that he should be despite winning 31 games that year for a flag winner. He was last seen in two relief appearances with the 1920 Tigers and also allowed no home runs in 173 innings to hitters in his rookie year 14 years earlier. Who is he?

Jack Coombs, a 31-game winner (in 353 innings) with the 1910 World Champion A's.

He finished his 10-year career, mostly spent in the pen, with a 33–26 won-lost log, a 3.47 ERA, and 187 saves. A pedestrian career in all, except for a stretch in the middle of it when he notched a record 82 consecutive successful saves. Who is he?

Eric Gagne. His 152 saves over the space of only three seasons is also a record.

Who was the last hurler to complete as many as 20 games in a season?

Fernando Valenzuela logged exactly 20 complete games for the 1986 Dodgers when he went 21–11, his lone 20-win season. The most recent hurler to complete as many as 15 games was Curt Schilling in 1998.

Who is the only pitcher in major-league history to awaken as late as the morning of September 16 with fewer than 15 wins but finish the regular season as a 20-game winner? This will seem to many as if it must be a nineteenth-century pitcher who came on late in the season to win as many as six games by pitching every other day and perhaps even every day for stretches. But it is actually a post-1900 rookie.

There once was a rookie 20-game winner that did not win Rookie of the Year honors despite also winning the first World Series game ever played in Cleveland Municipal Stadium that year and later saving the final Series game, the last time to date that Cleveland was victorious in the final official game of the season. All those clues should be ample to yield the name Gene Bearden and the year 1948.

What 200-game winner one year pitched for the 7th-place team in an 8-team league, posted a woeful 5.08 ERA, gave up 30 home runs, and yet reached the charmed circle when he beat the White Sox' Thornton Lee on the closing day of the season for his 20th win and league-leading 31st complete game? It was not his only 20-win season. Who was he, and what was his team that year?

Bobo Newsom of the 1938 St. Louis Browns. Usually found on teams buried deep in the second division, he was also a member of the flag-winning 1940 Tigers and 1947 Yankees.

The 1880 season brought the first two perfectos in major-league history when Lee Richmond and John Ward both fashioned nine-inning games where no baserunners reached base. There had been an earlier professional perfect game, however, by a Hall of Fame pitcher, who was the first in history to win 300 major-league games. In 1880, this same pitcher lost a chance to hurl yet a third perfecto that season in a game where he was responsible for no baserunners, but his Buffalo teammates made six errors behind him! Who was he?

On August 20, 1880, at Buffalo, Bisons ace Jim Galvin topped Worcester's Fred Corey, 1–0, on a wet and muddy field despite there being six errors behind him—the most ever by a team behind a pitcher who was otherwise perfect. Galvin had to overcome two boots each by second baseman Davy Force and third baseman Dan Stearns, plus a dropped throw by first baseman Dude Esterbrook and a fumbled grounder by shortstop Mike Moynahan, who was making his big-league debut. Esterbrook atoned for his miscue by tripling home outfielder Joe Hornung for the game's lone run. Galvin had earlier fashioned a perfect game for independent Pittsburgh against the Cass Club of Detroit in 1876.

Who are the only two pitchers since World War II to win 25 games in a season more than once? They are also the only two 25-game winners since World War II to allow fewer than 8.0 baserunners per nine innings pitched in at least one of their 25-win seasons.

Sandy Koufax and Juan Marichal, three times each. Koufax actually allowed under 8.0 baserunners per nine innings in two of his 25-win seasons.

To pique fading fan interest toward the end of the Deadball Era, baseball experimented with expanding the World Series to the best 5-of-9 games for three seasons. It offered an opportunity, given travel days, for a pitcher working on short rest to make four starts and win four games, but none of the potential nine-game Series went the distance. Who was the lone hurler during the brief 5-of-9 experiment to join the rarified list to win three games in a World Series?

In 1920, Cleveland's Stan Coveleski topped Brooklyn in Games 1, 4, and 7 to bring the Indians their first World Championship, 5 games to 2. Coveleski's games were relatively uneventful, but in Game 5, at Cleveland's League Park, three remarkable Series firsts occurred.

Before reading on, test yourself on whether you know what these three firsts were.

Cleveland's Jim Bagby, the Tribe's lone 30-game winner ever, hit the first Series home run by a pitcher; Indians outfielder Elmer Smith smacked the first Series grand slam; and Cleveland second baseman Bill Wambsganss turned the lone unassisted triple play in postseason history to date.

Excluding active pitchers, who is the only hurler with a minimum of 300 career starts to surrender fewer hits per nine innings than Sandy Koufax?

We can add that he is the only one with a minimum of 700 career starts to surrender fewer hits per nine innings than Walter Johnson and is second in career starts only to Cy Young. Moreover, he was the first to break Johnson's career strikeout record. Yes, it's Nolan Ryan. The strikeout king set dozens of records in the course of his long career, but one that is seldom noted came in 1987.

Don't read on until giving yourself a shot at recalling what his 1987 record was.

His .333 winning percentage that year after he went 8–16 for Houston is the lowest ever by a league ERA leader.

Remember we consider the National Association (1871–1875) to have been the first major league. With that caveat, name the only hurler to collect two 20-win seasons in major-league play but never win 20 games in any of the following major leagues: National Association, National League, American Association, Union Association, American League, and Players League.

So then, what's left? Right. The 1914–1915 Federal League. Sixteen different pitchers bagged 20-win seasons in the FL, including several big names like Chief Bender and Claude Hendrix. But only one did it in both years the Federal League was considered a major circuit. Now win a new car with his name. Right again. Gene Packard. Would he have logged even one 20-win season had he not jumped the Reds to join the FL? Probably not.

Ever since pitch counts began being scrupulously charted, the record for the lowest pitch count in a postseason contest by a starting pitcher who went the necessary five innings to collect the win is 54. It belongs to a hurler who won the 7th and deciding game via a combined shutout in a recent LCS. Who is he?

Surely you remember—you probably even watched it or at least part of it. Charlie Morton of the Astros in the decisive Game 7 of the 2017 ALCS. Long before pitch counts became a concern, in Game 3 of the 1924 World Series at the Polo Grounds, Giants starter Hugh McQuillan got the win as per the official scorer's decision, permissible at that time even though he went just 3 ⅔ innings and gave up two earned runs rather than reliever Rosy Ryan, who came in with the Giants ahead 3–1, gave up the second run charged to McQuillan, and then two of his own in 4 ⅔ innings pitched in the 6–4 Giants win over Washington. McQuillan faced only 17 batters, left with the bases loaded, and gave up five walks and two hits so it's quite likely he delivered more than 54 pitches. He did not leave with an injury as he pitched in relief and got a save just two days later facing six batters. Note that in the 2014 World Series, Jeremy Guthrie of the Kansas City Royals became the first starter since McQuillan to get a win after recording no more than 15 outs and no strikeouts in his Game 3, 3–2 win over the Giants but delivered more than 54 pitches.

The only pitcher since 1901 to win 20 games for a last-place team in a season that called for fewer than 140 games did it with a club that won only 52 times in 128 decisions. The abbreviated schedule alone should tell you the year it happened.

In 1918, Scott Perry went 20–19 with the cellar-dwelling 1918 A's. Those 20 wins represented half his career total of 40.

In the blasphemous 1994 strike season, Greg Maddux of the Braves led all pitchers in innings pitched with 202 and also led in complete games with 10. Whose record for fewest innings pitched in a season by the ML leader that called for a schedule of at least 60 games did he miss breaking by a third of an inning?

No, no, don't say you went all the way back to the war-shortened 1918 season when all you needed to do was transpose that year's final two digits. Yep, it was in 1981, our other infamous strike-abbreviated season, that the leader in innings pitched, Dennis Leonard of the Kansas City Royals, toed the rubber in just 201 ⅔ innings. Which were quite a lot considering how few games the Royals actually played (just 103). The 1981 campaign was actually Leonard's seventh consecutive 200+ innings season. Although just thirty years old at the time, he never again pitched enough innings to qualify for an ERA title.

While we're talking about 1981, a certain pitcher that year achieved the dubious distinction of being the only hurler to date to lose three games in a single postseason matchup—and in a 6-game World Series no less! Unintentionally, that is. Lefty Williams of the infamous Black Sox purposely lost a trio in the rigged 1919 Fall Classic. Our man, a Yankee of course if you know even a smidgen of World Series history, dropped Games 3, 4 and 6—but not without a fight.

Oh, please, not Joe Frazier. This was George Frazier, the long, tall relief pitcher. He was 0–1 in the 1981 regular season with a very neat 1.63 ERA and logged a perfect 0.00 ERA and 1–0 record in his lone ALCS outing against the Oakland A's, in contrast to his 17.18 ERA in his three World Series appearances.

And shall we also dally a moment longer on low totals by innings pitched leaders? In 2012, the Colorado Rockies went through 27 pitchers in the course of losing 98 games, 18 of whom notched 40 or more innings. The work was spread so thin that only one hurler worked as many as 100 innings. The leader's total of 113, spread over 24 starts (or less than five innings per start), is the lowest number of innings pitched by a club leader on a team that played its full schedule going all the way back to 1871. Given that, it should be not at all shocking to learn the Rockies' staff registered nary a complete game in 2012, let alone a shutout. Since this occurred not long ago, it shouldn't be impossible to remember the Rockies' ace in 2012 with six wins in 13 decisions to go with his 113 innings pitched. Or should it? How about the middle reliever who led the staff with eight wins to go with just two losses and its closer who labored valiantly to net 31 saves and a neat 1.127 WHIP?

The leader in innings pitched was Jeff Francis. Rex Brothers led the 2012 Rockies in wins with eight, and Rafael Betancourt served as the club's thankless closer. All the more bizarre, the Rockies that year not only had zero pitchers that won in double figures—they also had no double-digit losers! Alex White, Drew Pomeranz, and Jeremy Guthrie all tied for the lead in losses with nine.

In 1876, when Mark Twain was forty-one, he published a novel in America that had been published earlier in England and has been a popular read in both nations (and across the globe) ever since. For an obvious reason, its title character lodged in the minds of some baseball observers seven years later when the National League's Cleveland Blues summoned a novice replacement for their injured staff ace, Jim McCormick, from the local sandlots. Unfortunately, the rookie's name did not stick in the minds of any members of Cleveland's brass after he went just 4–10 in 15 starts and 2 relief appearances. No one at the time had a clue just how deceptive that won-lost record really was. He was allowed to disappear into the minors the following year and then depart from the professional baseball scene altogether when a better paying job beckoned. Which was unfortunate, for years later when people began taking into account such things as the fewest hits allowed per nine innings by pitchers, it came to light that the Blues' frosh lefty in 1883 was the only qualifier in all of major-league history to top his loop in fewest hits allowed per nine innings in his lone big-league season.

The obvious reason was that the lefty's name was Sawyer—Will Sawyer—and the popular novel was, of course, *Tom Sawyer*. Will put together quite a prosperous life after he left the diamond sport behind. His bio can be found online and is well worth reading.

In 2008, the Yankees' Mike Mussina joined a very small club when he racked up 20 wins in his final season. In the process, he nearly set a new record for the fewest innings hurled by a 20-game winner when he clocked only 200 ⅓ frames. Only two pitchers in all of history prior to Mussina logged 20-win campaigns in fewer than 200 innings. Who were they?

The first to do it was rookie Bob Grim of the Yankees in 1954 in 199 innings. The second was Pedro Martínez 48 years later with the 2002 Red Sox in 199 ⅓ innings. In the decade since Mussina's effort, however, five more hurlers have won 20 games despite pitching fewer than 200 innings, with Blake Snell the most auspicious. In 2018, Snell won 21 games in a record-low 180 ⅔ innings for the Tampa Bay Rays.

Prior to Bob Grim's 1954 season, the record for the fewest innings hurled by a 20-game winner was seventy-four years old. Back in 1880, a right-hander with the pennant-winning Chicago White Stockings snared 21 wins and 22 complete games in just 24 starts and 210 ⅓ innings in his first full major-league season. Who was he?

Fred Goldsmith, part of the first pitching staff to showcase two 20-game winners in 1880. The other was Chicago rookie Larry Corcoran. To his dying day, Goldsmith fought to receive credit for inventing the curveball. His case has largely fallen on deaf ears for over a century now.

What 200-game winner finished with a .660 career winning percentage (203–105), hurled almost twice as many complete games as any other pitcher during his peak 10-year period, and yet never appeared in a World Series?

The late Roy Halladay, the author of the only postseason no-hitter except Don Larsen's perfect game. It came unfortunately in a League Division Series against Cincinnati rather than a World Series. Halladay labored for most of his career with uninspiring Toronto teams before joining the Phillies where he garnered his lone taste of postseason action before back trouble idled him. In his peak 10-year period, 2002–2011, he collected 63 complete games, 30 more than CC Sabathia, the runner-up during that span.

The save did not become an official stat until 1969. What hurler became the first in history to notch 200 saves that same year? Most of them were, of course, retrospective.

Hoyt Wilhelm finished the 1969 campaign with 211 saves after beginning it with 197, all of them retrospective.

At the conclusion of the 1969 season once retrospective saves were compiled, 14 pitchers ranging from Hoyt Wilhelm with 211 to Firpo Marberry with 101 were credited with 100 or more career saves. Who were the four members of the list at that time that had zero complete games to their credit? All were among the standout relievers in the 1960s, but none are in the Hall of Fame.

Ron Perranoski, Dick Radatz, John Wyatt, and Don McMahon.

Last seen in the majors with the 1941 Boston Braves and first seen more than a decade earlier in an Indians uniform, he is the only pitcher to date to surrender more than 1,000 career walks, post fewer than 1,000 career strikeouts, and finish with a .600+ career winning percentage. Who is he?

He also holds many pitchers' batting and slugging records and in 1948 won a minor-league batting title after his major-league days were behind him. The answer is Wes Ferrell, who held a .601 winning percentage. A distant second to him, given the same parameters, is Tommy Byrne with a .552 winning percentage.

The holder of the record for most innings pitched in a season without making a starting appearance (208 ⅓) also ranks second on the same list with 179 innings.

It's Mike Marshall. He also holds both the NL and AL records for most appearances in a season, with 106 games pitched with the Dodgers 1974 and 90 games pitched with the Twins in 1979, including one start on August 18 against the Yankees. In 1974, Marshall pitched 208 ⅓ innings in relief, going 15–12 with 21 saves.

Can you name the other four relievers to qualify for an ERA crown without making a start?

Bob Stanley (1982), Bill Campbell (1976), Eddie Fisher (1965), and the first to do it: Hoyt Wilhelm in 1952.

The only player to lead his league in winning percentage (29–9, .763) and score 100 or more runs (102) in the same season, many of them compiled at other positions, is also the first pitcher to appear in five World's Series. Knowing that he appeared in World's Series competition with the same team in two different leagues should be more than enough to summon forth this early-day great whose gravestone identifies him as the most versatile major leaguer prior to Babe Ruth.

In 1887, Bob Caruthers led the American Association in winning percentage and tallied 102 runs with the AA champion St. Louis Browns. Sold to Brooklyn after that season, he appeared in World's Series play with Brooklyn in 1889 against the National League champion New York Giants and then again in 1890 against Louisville of the American Association after Brooklyn fled the AA after the 1889 season and joined the NL. Previously, Caruthers had appeared in postseason play in the three consecutive seasons (1885–1887) with St. Louis.

What 200-game winner that pitched in five games in 1945 with his hometown Tigers as an eighteen-year-old southpaw was the last member of a World War II (1942–1945) championship club to be active in the majors?

Billy Pierce. He finished his career in the 1964 Giants' bullpen with a perfect 3–0 record and a 2.20 ERA in 34 games. Stan Musial barely missed tying Pierce for this feat. He retired after the 1963 season after winning World Championships with the 1942 and 1944 Cardinals.

The most recent southpaw to register a 30-win season in the National League is also the most recent member of his franchise to be a 30-game winner since it joined the NL in 1887.

Frank Killen of Pittsburgh, in 1896. A year earlier right-hander Pink Hawley won 31 games for the Pirates. The closest the Corsairs have come to a 30-game winner since was right-hander Jack Chesbro with 28 wins in 1902. However, before Pittsburgh joined the National League, the club was a member of the American Association from 1882–1887. Prior to the 1885 season Pittsburgh acquired left-hander Ed Morris from the disbanding Columbus Buckeyes. Morris proceeded to win 39 games in 1885 and 41 in 1886; his 80 victories are the most ever by a left-hander over a two-year span.

Who is the only pitcher to lead both the NL and AL in shutouts in the same season?

CC Sabathia started the 2008 season with the Cleveland Indians (AL) and went 6–8, with two shutouts (enough to tie with seven others for the AL lead) before he was traded in July to the Milwaukee Brewers (NL) where he went 11–2 and bagged three shutouts to tie teammate Ben Sheets for the NL lead. Sabathia, with five total shutouts, obviously led the majors in shutouts that season.

Name the first pitcher to make the Hall of Fame solely for his major-league achievements despite logging a losing career record.

His career mark was 114–118. But he also had 341 saves, a career record at the time of his retirement in 1985. Yes, it was Rollie Fingers. Bruce Sutter and Trevor Hoffman have since joined Fingers in the Hall with losing records, as has Hank O'Day whose contributions were largely as an umpire. Satchel Paige made the Hall prior to Fingers with a losing record in the majors, but his selection was almost entirely for his Negro League contributions.

Frank Lary was nicknamed "The Yankee Killer," but among pitchers with a minimum of 20 decisions against the Yankees, he does not have the best winning percentage. What hurler went 17–5 for a .773 winning percentage against the Yankees and went on to log a perfect 1.000 winning percentage once he became a member of the Yankees?

Too much information? Probably. But it's sort of a trick question. All of Babe Ruth's wins against the Yankees came with strong Boston teams against less than stellar Yankees clubs. In 1917 alone, he went 5–0 versus the Yanks and yielded only one home run against them in 207 ⅔ innings. Upon the Babe joining the Yankees in 1920, it was hardly as a pitcher. In his long tenure with the Bombers, he went 5–0 in periodic starts, most of them well advertised in advance to draw large crowds.

The record for the most relief decisions in a season is 31. It belongs to a Tigers bullpenner who went 17–14 in 1974 in 59 games. Name him.

John Hiller, who also had 13 saves. The previous year, Hiller set a season record for saves (38) that lasted until Dan Quisenberry broke it a decade later. Second to Hiller with 27 decisions (12–15) is Mike Marshall of the 1974 Dodgers. Hiller is also second in relief wins in a season with 17 to the Pirates' Roy Face, who netted 18 in 1958 before suffering his only loss of the season in his final decision.

Several hurlers have won as many as 30 games in a season since the American League emerged as a major league in 1901 but not made the Hall of Fame. Who leads the pack with 34 wins in his landmark campaign?

Joe Wood, with 34 wins for the 1912 Red Sox.

The record holder for the most relief losses in a season set his mark of 16 the year after he was instrumental in stopping Pete Rose's record-tying NL hitting streak at 44 games. Who is he?

Gene Garber of the 1979 Atlanta Braves.

Trever Miller broke in with the 1996 Tigers as a start-ing pitcher. When he next appeared in the majors two years later it was as a reliever with the Astros. And a reliever he remained until the end of his career in 2011. What record did Miller set by a wide margin in 2007 while with the Astros?

He appeared in 76 games without registering a decision. Prior to Miller, no one had appeared in as many as 50 games without a decision. Miller's record lasted all of one year. In 2012, while splitting the season between the Marlins and the Dodgers, Randy Choate set the present record of 80 hill appearances without a decision.

But Trever Miller did have one save in 2007. Who currently holds the season record for the most appearances without a decision or a save?

Peter Moylan of the Kansas City Royals, with 79 in 2017. If you nailed both Choate and Moylan, you belong in a league of your own. If you know that the record held by Moylan prior to expansion belonged to Eddie Erautt of the Reds with a mere 30 appearances in 1951, I want to be in your league. In any case, there are many questions of this type that further illustrate how different pitcher usage is nowadays as compared to pre-expansion.

Who was the only rookie to win three games in a best-of-seven World Series? All of his 194 career wins came with the same team.

Babe Adams, with the 1909 Pirates.

Who is the only hurler to sandwich three consecutive seasons in which he saved 40 or more games between two separate strings of three or more consecutive seasons in which he started 30 or more games?

Dennis Eckersley and Hoyt Wilhelm are both lame guesses. It was John Smoltz, who returned to the Braves in 2001 mainly as a reliever after sitting out the previous season with an injury. In his four seasons in the pen he racked up 20, 68, 55, and 61 saves, respectively, before resuming his original role as a starter in 2005.

5***** When Sandy Koufax won 27 games in 1966 before his arthritic elbow forced his early retirement, whose record did he break for the most wins by a pitcher in his final big-league season? Start with the clues that banned pitchers like Jim Devlin, Lefty Williams and Eddie Cicotte are excluded and our man here, like Koufax, was a southpaw.

Before licking your chops and quickly gravitating to the somewhat obscure Henry Schmidt who won 22 games as a rookie with Brooklyn in 1903 and never appeared in the majors again, fair warning: You need to harken back even farther. The record belongs to a southpaw who twice won more than 35 games in a season before slipping to 8–30 and 4–17 campaigns that were further marred by frequent fines and suspensions for prodigious drinking episodes. In 1890, his sixth and final year in the show, he held it together to win 23 games (some historians say 24) for the American Association St. Louis Browns before being dropped from the team late in the season. For reasons still not fully understood, he never got another big top offer even though his alcoholism seemed finally under control. His name was Tom Ramsey, nicknamed Toad, and we encourage even casual fans of the game to read more about him.

Quicksilver Sluggers

None of the hitters we'll encounter here were recognized during their careers as Silver Sluggers, but all had moments when they accomplished unique or record-breaking slugging feats.

Mickey Mantle is the most recent non-Silver Slugger with a minimum of 4,000 career plate appearances to compile both a slugging average of .510 or better and an on-base percentage of .410 or better on a sub-.300 career batting average. Only one other slugger can make the same claim. What's more, he did it on a .286 career batting average, whereas Mantle's was .298, and just 189 home runs compared to the Mick's 536. Your clue is his career was winding down when the Mick's was just starting.

Charlie Keller is the man. Would it have helped if we'd thrown in that he spent most of his career with the Yankees even though he and Mickey were never teammates? Probably. But by not doing so we hope to encourage you to look at Keller's body of work.

Were it not for a congenital back problem that reduced him to pinch-hitting duty in the latter third of his career, there is a possibility he would now have a plaque in Cooperstown.

The last batsman to win a league home run crown with a total of less than 10 did it in his poorest full season in the majors, hitting just .232 with a .696 OPS. Who is he?

In 1918, Gavvy Cravath of the Phillies led the NL with eight home runs on a .232 batting average, 55 points below his career average. It was the fifth dinger crown he had either won or shared, but arguably the worst season ever by a home run king. The following year Cravath spotted himself judiciously while serving as the Phils' player-manager and hammered 12 home runs in just 241 at-bats to win his sixth home run crown. His slugging that year earned him the distinction of being the last home run king who did not take enough swings to be a batting title qualifier.

Who are the only two league home run champs to be officially banned from baseball?

George Hall, the winner of the very first National League home run crown in 1876, was barred the following year for taking part in the Louisville Scandal, which emanated from a post-season investigation that determined that Hall and two of his Louisville teammates, Jim Devlin and Al Nichols, had conspired to throw the 1877 NL pennant to Boston. A fourth member of the Kentucky club, Bill Craver, was barred on general principals. Over 40 years later, Heinie Zimmerman, the 1912 NL home run king, was tossed from the game after the 1919 season for allegedly participating in fixing games. Not the sharpest knife in the drawer, Zimmerman had come to the New York Giants from the Cubs in 1916 and by 1919 had fallen in with the nefarious Hal Chase, reputedly an inveterate game fixer but somehow never caught with the goods on him. Chase, the 1915 Federal League home run king, also left the majors after the 1919 season even though he escaped being formally banned.

What Expos second baseman is the only player in history to collect 50 or more doubles in a season but post both a sub-.400 slugging average and sub-.700 OPS?

Mark Grudzielanek, with 54 doubles, a .384 SA, and just a .690 OPS with the 1997 Expos. He never again approached 50 doubles in a season but finished with a career .289 batting average and a .725 OPS to go along with 2,040 hits.

What first baseman set a record, since broken, for the most doubles in a season but nonetheless logged a sub-.500 slugging average when he notched just four homers and three triples to go with his 64 two-baggers?

George Burns of the 1926 Indians, who was also the winner of the American League MVP that season. His .494 slugging average that year is a record low by a batsman with 60 or more doubles. The following season Burns again racked up a ton of doubles (51) but slugged at just a .435 clip.

In his top season he set records for both the highest batting average and the most total bases by a qualifier who failed to homer all year. Later in his career he became the first to homer in the uniforms of all three New York City–based franchises. Who is he?

Seven years later to be exact. In 1897, Willie Keeler of the Baltimore Orioles hit .424 and compiled 304 total bases while going homerless. In 1904 Keeler, by then in his second season with the AL New York Highlanders, hit two home runs after going homerless the previous year with the club. Keeler had earlier homered with both the New York and Brooklyn NL franchises. Keeler's mark of 304 total bases in a homerless season has never been seriously threatened. In 1906, Nap Lajoie of the Cleveland Naps had 280 total bases in a homerless season, but no one else has come within 50 of Keeler's 1897 total.

The first man to smack two home runs in a modern World Series led all hitters in his lone postseason appearance with a .529 slugging average. Conversely, he also holds the all-time record for the highest season batting average by a qualifying batsman with a sub-.400 slugging average. His record-breaking season came in 1902 when he rapped .342 but compiled just a .397 SA.

Patsy Dougherty, in his rookie year with the Boston Americans. The following year he hit .331 for the Americans, capped by his World Series longball work that fall, and then never reached .290 again in his 10-year career.

His 12-year big-league career featured a rookie season in which he compiled a 1.004 OPS in 125 games but failed to win the NL Rookie of the Year Award, losing it in a disputed fashion to an Expos pitcher that won 18 games. His overall career stats included 538 walks, a mere 611 Ks, and 358 RBI to go with a .814 OPS but just 722 hits as he never again compiled a .300 batting average or more than 88 hits in a season after his rookie year. In 1975, after being traded to the Red Sox, he was the utility outfielder in a pasture that included rookie stars Fred Lynn, Dwight Evans, and Jim Rice. Facing him that fall were many of his teammates in his rookie season. Who is he? And... who is the long-forgotten Expos' pitcher that beat him out for the National League Rookie of the Year Award in 1970?

Bernie Carbo. The Expos' hurler was Carl Morton, who died of a heart attack at age thirty-nine. A notorious flake, Boston Carbo traveled on road trips with a stuffed gorilla named Mighty Joe Young seated beside him on the plane. His career highlight came in the 1975 World Series when his three-run pinch homer for the Sox in Game Six sent the contest into extra innings, setting the stage for Carlton Fisk's famous walk-off home run.

Two seasons after he became the oldest pitcher to hurl a shutout in the majors, at age forty-nine, he became the oldest player to notch an RBI when he beat out an infield hit that drove home Colorado runners from both second and third with two out. Who are we talking about?

Jamie Moyer, who returned to major-league duty with the 2012 Rockies after missing the 2011 season. In 2003, Moyer, then with the Mariners, became the only southpaw other than Warren Spahn to be a 20-game winner in the year he turned forty.

The first switch-hitter to win an AL MVP Award was Mickey Mantle. Mantle won three such awards and was a bona fide Silver Slugger had the award existed. The second switch-hitter to follow in Mantle's footsteps and cop an AL MVP Award was a frequent All-Star but never in the running for any slugging prizes. Who is he?

Vida Blue, who in 1971 went 24–8 for the Oakland A's but hit just .118 in only 102 at-bats.

Among all players in major-league history who finished with a minimum of 5,000 career at-bats and a batting average of .310 or better, the lowest career OPS (.740) belongs to a Hall of Famer who played in what most historians believe to have been the first major-league game.

Deacon White, with 6,624 at-bats, a .312 BA, and a .740 OPS. White caught for Cleveland when it faced the Fort Wayne team in the National Association's opening game in 1871.

In 2010, Mark Reynolds of the Diamondbacks scored 79 runs while hitting .198. Whose record for the most runs scored in a season on a sub-.200 batting average did he fall short of breaking?

In 1940, Yankees shortstop Frank Crosetti scored 84 runs despite hitting just .194 to set the current record. Prior to 1940, the record belonged to Germany Smith of the 1890 Brooklyn Bridegrooms who tallied 76 runs on a .191 batting average. Interestingly, both Crosetti and Smith not only were shortstops but also played on pennant winners during those seasons.

Who is the only Hall of Famer to win a home run crown in the American Association during its sojourn as a major league?

Dan Brouthers is a nice guess but incorrect. The answer is the only man to spend more than two seasons in the rebel AA and subsequently make the Hall of Fame solely for his playing skills, though not until 2000. Bid McPhee. McPhee's eight homers in 1886 made him the lone middle infielder to win an AA home run title.

In 1912, second baseman Morrie Rath, then with the White Sox, totaled just 19 RBI to go with his 104 runs scored. Who broke Rath's eighty-eight-year-old record for the fewest RBI in a season (17) by a player that scored 100 or more runs?

In 2000, Luis Castillo of the Marlins, also a second baseman, broke Rath's ancient record when he tallied 101 runs for the Marlins but logged just 17 RBI despite a .334 batting average.

Who is the only batsman to achieve double-digit totals in each extra-base hit department (doubles, triples, and home runs) and collect more triples than he had doubles and home runs combined?

This is much easier than it may at first appear. In 1912, out-fielder Chief Wilson of the Pirates bagged a record 36 triples, six more than his combined total of 19 doubles and 11 home runs.

Chief Wilson's 19 doubles in 1912 were 17 less than his record-setting 36 triples, but he does not hold the record for the largest disparity by a hitter with more triples in a season than doubles. The slugger who does is better known for being the first in history to compile four consecutive home run crowns. Name him.

In 1897, Harry Davis of the Pirates slammed 28 triples and only 10 doubles, a record-setting difference of 18 that will almost certainly never be topped. Soon thereafter, Davis's career foundered until he joined Philadelphia in the upstart American League in 1901. Serving as the A's first baseman, he won four consecutive AL home run titles between 1904–1907.

Take a moment now to ponder who tied Davis's record when he became the second ALer to bag four home run crowns in a row.

No, not the Babe. It was another A's infielder who teamed with Davis early in his career. Home Run Baker, in 1911–1914. Baker tied Tris Speaker for the crown in 1912.

Who were the first two hitters to assemble seasons in which they led both the National League and American League in slugging average?

Furthermore, they both led their respective leagues in slugging in 1966. It was Frank Robinson in the AL and Dick Allen in the NL.

Name the first player to win two National League home run crowns in the twentieth century.

You deserve a silver star if you said Tim Jordan. The Brooklyn first baseman paced the NL in four baggers in both 1906 and 1908 with a total of 12 in each season. Jordan also has another distinction: His 32 career homers are the fewest since 1901 by a multiple home run king.

Prior to expansion in 1961, who held the record for the highest OPS by a qualifier with a sub-.250 batting average? Knowing he did it in his final season should give you a running start.

In 1947, after being sold by Detroit to Pittsburgh, Hank Greenberg had a portion of Forbes Field's left field sector named after him. Called "Greenberg Gardens," it immediately became the favorite target of Pittsburgh's sophomore slugger Ralph Kiner, but Greenberg also was given a boost, belting 25 home runs en route to a .885 OPS on just a .249 batting average in his final big-league season. No less than 18 of Greenberg's 25 jacks came in Forbes Field.

What player followed a season in which he hit .219 in 100 games with a season in which he became the first player in American League history to collect as many as 20 doubles, 20 triples, and 20 homers in the same season?

Jeff Heath, with the 1941 Indians. Had Heath had a season anywhere close to his 1941 campaign the previous year, the Tribe would almost unquestionably have won the 1940 pennant.

Which of the following sluggers never was an American League season leader in home run percentage per 100 at-bats? Bob Meusel, Charlie Keller, Wally Pipp, Luke Easter, Sam Crawford, or Nick Etten?

Sam Crawford.

Who are the only three sluggers to date with 400 or more career home runs on a sub-.250 career batting average?

Dave Kingman, with 442 home runs and a .236 BA; Darrell Evans, with 414 home runs on a .248 BA; and Adam Dunn, with 462 home runs and a .237 BA.

Prior to expansion in 1961, the record for most career home runs on a sub-.250 career batting average was held by what catcher with 164 home runs and a .243 BA? He appeared in his lone World Series after having his best season with a .288 BA and 24 home runs. His middle name was Wasal, which was his father's first name.

That last clue should help steer you to someone of Eastern European ethnicity. In this case, Andy Seminick, a member of the pennant-winning 1950 Phillies.

What player missed the American League batting title by one point in his first year with the St. Louis Browns (after arriving in a trade) when he logged a career-high .989 OPS? Had he won the title that season he would have been the last Brownie to do so before the club moved to Baltimore.

Heinie Manush, whose .378 BA in 1928 lost out to Goose Goslin's .379. Two years earlier, with the Tigers, Manush had won the AL batting crown with an identical .378 BA, but his OPS was four points lower.

In 1914, second baseman Eddie Collins of the Philadelphia A's won the AL batting crown with a .344 average under today's qualification rules, but some sources still award it to Ty Cobb. If Collins is considered the winner, it would be over 20 years before the AL batting title again went to a player with a sub-.350 BA—and again, it was a second baseman. Who was it, and what year did he do it?

Buddy Myer of the Washington Senators hit .349 in 1935 to beat out Cleveland's Joe Vosmik for the AL batting crown by one point on the last day of the season.

Besides Myer, four other players whose primary position was second base were undisputed AL batting champs between 1901 and expansion in 1961. Can you name all four?

Nap Lajoie in 1901, 1903, 1904, and 1910...sort of; Charlie Gehringer in 1937; Snuffy Stirnweiss in 1945; and Pete Runnels in 1960. Runnels is the one most often forgotten because he played first base in 1962 when he won his second batting title. Note that in 1954 the batting title awarded to Cleveland's Bobby Avila belonged to Ted Williams by today's qualification rules. Lajoie's 1910 crown is still credited by some sources to Ty Cobb.

In 1929, Tony Lazzeri of the Yankees racked up a .561 slugging average. Prior to then, only two American League second basemen had achieved seasons that included a .500 or better slugging average. One was Nap Lajoie, who had multiple .500+ slugging seasons in the AL. The other logged a .500 slugging on the nose in 1902 as a member of the soon-to-fold Baltimore Orioles. Three years earlier, he had set a rookie record that still stands while playing third base for a National League club that he jumped to when the AL declared itself a major league prior to the 1901 season. Who is he?

Jimmy Williams. In 1899, as a rookie with the Pirates, Williams cracked a frosh record 27 triples. After jumping to the AL Baltimore Orioles and switching to second base, Williams nailed 21 triples in 1901 and again in 1902, which remained the AL record for second basemen until Snuffy Stirnweiss broke it with 22 in 1945.

Who holds the record for most extra-base hits in a season excluding home runs? He had 64 doubles and 13 triples for a total of 77.

Sure, it would have helped if I'd added that he won a Triple Crown the following year. It was Joe Medwick in 1936, when he had 95 extra-base hits altogether including his 18 home runs. In 1936, Medwick had 97 extra-base hits—his career high—when his Triple Crown slash line was .374/31/154.

What is the only team in ML history to feature three players with 40 or more home runs but only one player with as many as 100 RBI? It was also the first team ever to have two sluggers park 40 home runs with fewer than 100 RBI, as well as the first with three 40-homer men.

The 1973 Atlanta Braves. Darrell Evans had 41 homers and 104 RBI, but Hank Aaron knocked home only 96 runs to go with his 40 homers while second baseman Davey Johnson clubbed 43 homers and 99 RBI. The only other team to date with two 40+-homer men that fell short of 100 RBI was the 2015 Angels with Albert Pujols and Mike Trout.

In the twentieth century, what slugger led the majors with 19 home runs in a season, all of which came in his home park? Amazingly, that same season his team's entire pitching staff gave up only 16 jacks all year in that same park.

Gavvy Cravath again, in 1914, playing in the Baker Bowl where the right-field fence down the line was only 279 feet from home plate. It needs to be noted that Cravath was a right-handed hitter.

In 1961, what catcher became the first son of a former big leaguer to hit 20 or more homers in a season?

Earl Douglas Averill, the son of Howard Earl Averill, with 21 dingers for the expansion Los Angeles Angels in 1961. He was also the first son of a Hall of Famer to do it.

What Hall of Famer led the NL with a 1.036 OPS in 1936 even though he did not finish among the top five in batting average?

Mel Ott of the Giants. Second to him in OPS at 1.018 was Dolph Camilli of the Phillies who did not finish among the top five either. Cardinal Johnny Mize was 3rd at .979 and Pirate Paul Waner, the batting leader, was 4th with a .965 OPS.

Name the only eligible player not in the Hall of Fame whose career ended prior to the 1994 strike after he tabulated over 1,000 runs, over 1,000 RBI, over 300 home runs, over a .500 career slugging average, and over 1,700 games played but will have to be voted into the Hall by the Veterans' Committee if he is ever to be enshrined.

Dick Allen. Please join us in wishing him luck.

What slugger failed to win a home run crown in either league even though he compiled more total home runs that year than anyone else in the majors?

Mark McGwire in 1997 hit 34 homers for the Oakland A's and 24 with the St. Louis Cardinals after he was dealt to the National League for a total of 58.

Which of the following sluggers at no point during their playing days held the record for most career home runs in the National League? Note that there may be more than one answer. George Hall, Charley Jones, Cap Anson, Sam Thompson, Gavvy Cravath, Rogers Hornsby, Johnny Mize, or Mel Ott?

Cravath and Mize, even though both won multiple home run crowns.

5***** Prior to 1920, a walk-off home run was not considered a home run unless the batter himself represented the winning run. Otherwise it was scored as a single, double, or triple depending on how many men were on base at the time it was hit and how many runs were needed to win the game, which could only be won on such a hit by a one-run margin. On July 11, 1920, at Crosley Field, Cincinnati Reds first baseman Jake Daubert became the first beneficiary of the rule change when a ball he hit into the center-field bleachers against the Boston Braves in the bottom of the ninth with runners on first and second was counted as a home run even though the score was 3–3 at the time. It still is in the record books as a home run.

But, strangely enough, if the situation had been identical in every way 11 years later, Daubert's hit would only have been a double even though it ended up in the exact same spot in the center-field bleachers. Why so?

Daubert's hit in 1920 made it into the stands on the first bounce. Prior to the 1931 season, the NL adopted the rule already in effect in the AL that a ball that did not arrive in the stands in fair territory on the fly was no longer a home run.

Great Hitting Feats

The most recent National Leaguer to hit .390 or better for a full season was Tony Gwynn of the Padres with .394 in the strike-shortened 1994 campaign. The last American Leaguer to do so was Kansas City's George Brett, who finished at .390 on the nose in 1980. Prior to 1980, who was the last batsman to hit .390 or better but fall short of the .400 mark?

I know, I know. You were all set to blurt out Ted Williams in 1941 until I added that last sentence. The answer is Al Simmons of the Athletics, who led the American League with a .390 mark in 1931. The previous season, Brooklyn's Babe Herman became the last National Leaguer to do it prior to Gwynn when he ripped .393.

If the present-day rules (including those for, but not restricted to, determining batting title winners) had been in effect throughout major-league history, which of the following players would have won at least one more batting title than he is now credited with? Note that there are several others as well not on this list. Hugh Duffy, Paul Waner, Ted Williams, Rod Carew, Pete Browning, Taft Wright, Tito Francona, Edd Roush, Johnny Dickshot, Joe DiMaggio, Eddie Collins, or Jake Beckley.

Pete Browning, in 1886; Ted Williams, in 1954; Eddie Collins, in 1914; and Edd Roush, in 1918. Browning's Louisville teammate, pitcher-first baseman Guy Hecker, hit .341 to Browning's .340 but had only 378 plate appearances, short of the number presently needed to be a qualifier in 1886. In 1914, Ty Cobb outhit Eddie Collins by 24 points but had only 414 plate appearances and 345 at-bats. In 1918, Roush cost himself the batting title by triggering a successfully protested game when he juggled a fly ball; once stats from the game were thrown out (Roush had gotten two hits in the contest), Zack Wheat won the batting title. Williams had only 386 at-bats in 1954 but 526 plate appearances, more than the number needed that year after the present rule was enacted.

When Ichiro Suzuki amassed a record 262 hits in 2004, he batted a sizzling .372. Two years later, who set the current record for the lowest batting average by a 200-hit man when he rapped just .292 despite collecting a league-leading 204 hits?

Cubs outfielder Juan Pierre in 2006, his first season with the Bruins. In his 14-year career, Pierre had four 200-hit seasons but never had a season in which he compiled as many as 300 total bases. He finished with just 18 career home runs in 7,525 at-bats. Among all players with a minimum of 7,500 career at-bats, only Don Kessinger (14) and Larry Bowa (15) have fewer homers.

Both were middle infielders. Pierre leads all outfielders and first basemen on this list.

Ichiro Suzuki holds not only the current record for the most hits in a season but also the most consecutive seasons with 200 hits. Except for the outlier 1887 season when four strikes were allotted hitters and four players, given an extra strike, compiled 200 bona fide hits, who is the only player to register a 200-hit season prior to the pitching distance being lengthened to its present distance in 1893? He once won a batting title but not in the year he collected a pre-1893 record 205 hits (again, 1887 excepted).

Believe it or not, it was a shortstop. Jack Glasscock, with the 1889 Indianapolis Hoosiers of the National League. He won the NL batting title the following year after joining the New York Giants. Glasscock is considered by many to be the best all-around shortstop that played his entire career in the nineteenth century. Two factors weigh heavily against his Hall of Fame selection: He never played on a pennant winner, and he earned everlasting enmity from fellow players and a number of influential sportswriters when he reneged on a pledge to join the popular Players League in 1890 after previously deserting Cleveland in 1884 by jumping to the unpopular rebel Union Association.

The Atlanta NL franchise has occupied three different cities since its inception in Boston in 1871 and was blessed (or cursed) with innumerable nicknames before it finally settled permanently on the Braves. Who will always hold the single-season record for the most hits in a Boston Braves uniform?

Tommy Holmes, with 224 in 1945. In addition, in 1945, he became the last home run king to date who logged fewer than 10 strikeouts (9). Hugh Duffy holds the all-time franchise season record with 237 hits on the strength of his massive year with the 1894 Bostons, then known as the Beaneaters.

After spending his entire career with the same team, he became the first ex-major leaguer to broadcast his team's home games. In 1919, he led the American League with 105 walks despite hitting just .234. Two years earlier, he led in walks while hitting just .228. Who was he?

Jack Graney, a career Indian and the first to play as many as 1,000 games as an outfielder with the Tribe.

Prior to expansion, who were the only two American League players that could make this claim? I was my franchise's career leader in home runs, OPS, and outfield assists.

Ken Williams and Babe Ruth. The Babe's team-leading stats were compiled, of course, with the Yankees; Williams's came with the St. Louis Browns, ancestors of the Baltimore Orioles.

Who is the only pitcher since World War II to collect as many as 800 career plate appearances and post a career OPS of .700 or better? His .705 mark is better than those of several Hall of Fame position players.

Don Newcombe. His .271 career average leads all post-World War II qualifiers among pitchers by a comfortable margin—Johnny Sain is second at .245. But Newk is only third in slugging average. His .367 slugging trails Bob Lemon (.386) and Earl Wilson (.369). Third on the OPS list behind Newcombe and Lemon is Mike Hampton (.650). Hampton leads contemporary pitchers by a wide margin in all offensive departments.

In 2017, Rockies outfielder Charlie Blackmon set a new all-time season record for the most RBI by a leadoff hitter with 104. Who holds the record for the fewest RBI in a season by a leadoff hitter playing a minimum of 162 games? Nothing easy about this one. The record is over 100 years old and belongs to a lefty-hitting center fielder who was one of Ty Cobb's original teammates on the Tigers and, from all reports, his archnemesis when he first joined Detroit. Why? Mostly because Tyrus was poised to take his job soon thereafter.

Jimmy Barrett of the 1904 Tigers collected just 31 RBI in the first year the schedule was permanently set at 154 games until expansion occurred. The Tigers played an incredible 10 tie games in 1904 and only 152 games to a decision for a total of 162, coincidentally the number played now. Barrett also had just 31 RBI out of the leadoff spot in 1903 when the schedule still called for just 140 games.

The only Hall of Fame position player to collect over 1,000 big-league at-bats before he hit his first career home run totaled more career RBI than Mickey Mantle. Seems impossible, but it's definitely true. Who is he?

The clues are sparse but enough to make it apparent this player had a long career and hit with power, albeit not customarily with home run power. He was one of the first great "scientific" hitters, using all fields depending on the situation and the opposition. His career began in 1871, but his first homer did not come until August 26, 1876, at Chicago against George Bradley of St. Louis, arguably the best pitcher in the game that year. His leading career victim was an even better pitcher, Charley Radbourn, whom he touched for eight of his 97 circuit clouts. Got it now? Cap Anson.

In his lone year as a batting titlist, he set a record for the fewest runs created per game by a league leader with just 6.97 despite topping the majors in triples that same season with 22. Who is he?

Snuffy Stirnweiss, in 1945.

Among all retired players with at least 4,000 career plate appearances that had a sub-.300 career batting average and also a sub-.500 career slugging average, the highest career OPS belongs to the record holder prior to 2017 for the most walks in a season by a rookie. Who is this vastly underrated batsman whose .902 career OPS is higher than nearly a third of the performers who have tabulated 500 career home runs?

Bill Joyce. His career only consisted of eight seasons and several were marred by injuries. He also lost the entire 1893 season—the first of several paradisiacal seasons for hitters after the pitching distance was increased—when he held out (to no avail) after being traded from Brooklyn to Washington. Joyce wound up in lowly Washington anyway in 1894. Even with the missing holdout season he would technically have fallen one year short of eligibility for the Hall of Fame regardless of how mammoth his

1893 campaign had been. Would an exception have been made for this man who quit the game on his own terms while still in his prime? We will never know if Cooperstown would now have a plaque honoring Joyce. His rookie record for walks, set in the 1890 Players League, amazingly held sway until it was broken in 2017 by Aaron Judge. No one alive ever saw him play, and few by the time the Hall of Fame opened its doors still remembered him. But he was one of the greatest players in the nineteenth century and quite likely the most valuable third baseman. His paramount misfortune: being traded to the New York Giants in 1896 and not after the 1892 season. Joyce in a Giants uniform in the mid-1890s while the team was among the top NL clubs would almost unquestionably have changed the course of baseball history.

Excluding suspected steroids users, who was the most recent player to achieve an OBP of .500 or better in a season and not win the batting title?

Babe Ruth did it no less than four times—1920, 1921, 1924, and 1926. Excepting Barry Bonds, the most recent hitter to do it was Mickey Mantle in 1957 when he hit .365 with a .512 OBP but finished second in both batting and OBP to Ted Williams (.388/.526).

In 1908, Ty Cobb won the AL bat crown with a .324 average, 42 points below his career BA. Who is the only other player to win a batting title with an average that was 25 points or more below his career BA, and what year did he do it? It should help to know he led his league in hitting again the following year with a BA two points below his career average.

In 1988, Tony Gwynn, a career .338 hitter, paced the National League with a .313 BA, exactly 25 points below his career average. He won again in 1989 with a .336 mark.

In 1947, his final ML season, a certain first baseman hit just .224 but logged a .401 on-base percentage and an .823 OPS in 142 games. Who is he?

Roy Cullenbine of the Detroit Tigers.

On March 29, 2018, who became the first player to lead off a game on Opening Day for two consecutive seasons with a home run when he took Cole Hamels deep with a home run at Texas's Arlington Park?

George Springer of the Astros. The previous year he victimized Seattle's Félix Hernández on April 3, Opening Day, at Houston's Minute Maid Park.

Who is the only pitcher to hit over .400 in season when he had a minimum of 100 plate appearances while serving as a pitcher?

Walter Johnson rapped .433 in 1925 in 107 plate appearances. His 1.033 OPS in 1925 is also a season record high for a pitcher. Johnson had hit a career high of .283 in 1924 before compiling his singular season the following year.

Who is the most recent member of the Cleveland Indians to win an American League batting title according to the current rules for qualification?

Although Bobby Avila in 1954 is still credited by many with the AL batting title, Ted Williams won it under current rules that make the major criterion for qualification the total number of plate appearances rather than at-bats. Williams had more than enough plate appearances but fewer than the 400 at-bats needed at the time. The last winner under current rules is Lou Boudreau in 1944, also the last player-manager to win a batting title. Note that historians who believe current qualification rules should prevail over custom and usage at the time of a feat or an event credit Williams with the 1954 AL batting crown.

What thirty-year-old rookie is the record-holder for most hits in a season in which he did not have enough plate appearances by current rules to qualify for the batting title? He hit .373 with 146 hits for a pennant winner.

In 1930, Cardinals rookie outfielder George Watkins played in 119 games and shared garden duty with both Chick Hafey and Showboat Fisher. Even though he had only 391 at-bats, he qualified for the NL batting crown by the rules then in effect which required only that a player appear in a minimum of 100 games. In 1959, Tito Francona of the Indians hit .363 with 145 hits, narrowly missing Watkins's record amount but had too few plate appearances to qualify for the title. In 1970, Pittsburgh outfielder Roberto Clemente also tabulated 145 hits to go with a .352 average but fell short of the number of plate appearances to be a title qualifier and would not have won even if the requisite number of plate appearances (all of them required to be hitless) had been added to his total.

Who is the only non-pitcher in major-league history to post a

.400 or better season batting average in a minimum of 100 at-bats and fail to qualify for a batting title? In his super year he had 155 plate appearances and hit .403.

In 1957, after spending most of the season in the minors, out-fielder Bob Hazle earned the nickname "Hurricane" after joining the Milwaukee Braves in time to appear in 41 games and log a 1.126 OPS. The following year, split between the Braves and Tigers, Hazle hit just .211 in 63 games and spent the rest of his career back in the minors. The only other title non-qualifier to challenge the .400 mark with as many as 100 at-bats was catcher Don Padgett of the 1939 Cardinals who hit .399 in 233 at-bats but appeared in only 92 games, eight short of the requisite number at that time for a qualifier.

Who is the appropriately named first baseman whose solo home run won the longest LDS game in major-league history?

At 12:02 a.m. on October 5, 2014, in a NL Division Series game at Washington, Giants first baseman Brandon Belt blasted a home run off Washington's Tanner Roark in the top of the 18th inning to put San Francisco ahead 2–1. Belt's "belt" enabled a 6-hour-and-23-minute game to come to a merciful end for TV viewers all across the country when the Nationals failed to score in the bottom of the frame and gave the Giants what proved to be an insurmountable 2–0 lead in the best-of-five series. Belt spent his eighth season in the majors in 2018 but has yet to hit as many as 20 homers in a season, a rarity in today's game—especially for a first baseman.

The 20-20-20 club (20 homers, 20 doubles, and 20 triples) currently has seven members, but the 20-20-20-20 club (20 homers, 20 doubles, 20 triples, and 20 stolen bases) has only four. The first to achieve this feat did it with the 1911 Cubs, the second did it with the New York Giants 46 years later, and there was then a 50-year hiatus before the third and fourth performers to do it both join the 20-20-20-20 club in the same season. Name all four men to reach this four-pronged milestone.

Frank Schulte in 1911, Willie Mays in 1957, and Curtis Granderson and Jimmy Rollins in 2007. Granderson and Rollins are also the only pair to join the 20-20-20 club in the same season.

In 2017, Charlie Blackmon claimed the 11th National League batting title won by a member of the Colorado Rockies in the 25 seasons since their inception in 1993. All 11 of the bat crowns were won by players who hit blatantly better in the Rockies' Coors Field home park than on the road. What player who compiled a slash line of .313/.400/.565 over a 17-year career owns a blistering .334/.426/.618 slash line for his 10 seasons as a member of the Rockies?

Larry Walker, who garnered his only three batting titles while serving with the Rockies. His BA was some .50 points lower during his time spent with the Expos and Cardinals. Walker is the poster boy among hitters who thrived with the Rockies but were only a cut or two above average in other uniforms. Had he spent his entire career with the Rockies, he almost certainly would now be in the Hall of Fame.

In hitter-happy 1930, only 11 batting title qualifiers (400 or more at-bats) in the National League hit below the league average of .303. One of the 11 nonetheless made the Hall of Fame. His .281 average in 1930 matched that of his team, which tied for last in the NL in batting. Who is he?

Rabbit Maranville of the Boston Braves.

At age thirty, Ty Cobb had a .370 career batting average with 5,795 at-bats. He suffered remarkably little decline after that. Who is the only batsman with a minimum of 3,000 at-bats when he turned thirty with a higher career batting average at that age than Cobb's?

By the time he turned thirty in 1903, Willie Keeler had compiled 1,955 hits and owned a .371 career BA. His average declined every year after that. In his eight remaining seasons, he hit a respectable .294, but his OPS was only .688.

Prior to the arrival of Mickey Mantle, who held the Yankees' record for most career hits by a switch-hitter? You get a generous clue that Mantle broke the club record in 1955, just his fifth season in the show.

Shortstop Mark Koenig, with a mere 636. Wally Schang, primarily a catcher, was the runner-up with 483. Through 1955, Schang was third, however, in career hits by an American League switch-hitter with 1,506.

Who is the most recent player to lead his league in both triples and home runs in the same season? He set career high totals in both departments that year, led both leagues in triples and homers, and collected 406 total bases—at the time the most by an American Leaguer since 1937.

In 1978, Jim Rice of the Red Sox paced the American League in triples with 15 and home runs with 46. He also had 15 triples in 1977 but never again bagged more than seven in a season.

Who broke Jack Crooks's 115-year-old record for the fewest hits in a season that included 130 or more walks?

The length of the record should be a huge clue that something very unique was afoot. In 1892, Crooks compiled 136 walks but just 95 hits while batting .213 for the St. Louis Browns, by then in the National League. After more than an entire century had elapsed, in 2007, Barry Bonds collected 132 walks but just 94 hits in hitting .276 for the San Francisco Giants. It was the final season of Bonds's reputedly late-career steroid-fueled power surge that sparked all kinds of odd record combinations and resulted in his becoming only the second batter in ML history to generate two seasons in which he walked 100 or more times while compiling less than 100 hits. His first had come the previous year in 2006.

What player won a batting title the year after he broke Howie Shanks's forty-year-old major-league record of 44 by scoring the fewest runs by an outfielder (42) with 500 or more at-bats? It was his lone hitting crown, and even though he never matched his hitting stats that year, he's in the Hall of Fame.

Al Kaline, in 1954, his rookie year with the Tigers. He topped the AL in batting the following year.

Whose career line reflects that he collected over 300 more RBI than he scored runs? In 1960, he set the current record for the fewest runs scored by a player with 100 or more RBI when he drove home 103 runs but tallied only 45 runs himself, 19 of them on his own round-trippers.

Vic Wertz, with the Red Sox. He never scored 100 runs in a season but logged five 100-RBI campaigns. In 1947, his rookie year with the Tigers, he scored 60 runs and drove in 44. Never again in his extraordinarily checkered 17-year career did he collect more tallies than he generated RBI.

*5***** Only once in history were batting titles in the same league won in consecutive years by players on last-place teams. Who were the two players and their teams, and who were their Hall of Fame managers?*

In 1915, Larry Doyle of the last-place Giants took the National League batting title under John McGraw. The following year, the NL crown was worn by the infamous Hal Chase under Christy Mathewson, who, in his first season as Cincinnati's player-manager, brought the Reds home tied with St. Louis for the NL cellar.

Memorable Teams

At the close of the 2017 season, even many pundits believed the Houston Astros had become the first franchise ever to win pennants in two different major leagues in the same century, but they were wrong. Why?

In 1889, the Brooklyn Bridegrooms won the American Association pennant. The American Association without question was a major league between 1882 and 1891. During the winter of 1889–1890, internal friction among AA owners led both the Bridegrooms and the Cincinnati Reds to abscond to the National League prior to the 1890 season. Sharp enough to sign almost their entire roster before they could be lost to Players League raiders, the Bridegrooms proved to be the class of the National League in 1890. They remain today the only team to win back-to-back pennants—not only in two different leagues, but without ever placing a single member of their cast—including manager Bill McGunnigle and team owner Charlie Byrne—in the Hall of Fame. Some historians also consider the Boston

Reds, who won the Players League pennant in 1890 and then took the American Association flag in 1891 with several key members of their 1890 crew still part of the club to have been the same franchise. But to purists they were not. Although they had the same team name and played in the same park, Congress Street Grounds, both their front office personnel and team composition were sufficiently different to mark them as two different franchises. Note that the Cincinnati Reds' and the St. Louis Cardinals' franchises have also won pennants in two different major leagues but not in the same century. Both won pennants in the American Association in the nineteenth century, but their first National League pennants did not arrive until 1919 and 1926, respectively. Likewise, the Brewers would not have qualified, as they won the NL pennant in 2018 since their AL pennant came in 1982.

What team had a record seven pitchers that posted win totals in double figures and none that lost more than eight games? Included was a 20-game winner, and the two leading losers were both Hall of Famers with eight and seven losses, respectively. Name the team, its two Hall of Fame hurlers, and take a point for each of the other five double-digit winners you can recall.

The 1939 Yankees, considered by many historians to be the best Yankees club of all-time if not the absolute best team ever. Not only did they have such a deep pitching staff that seven members contributed double-figure win totals but also had a rookie lefty, Marius Russo, who allowed just 6.67 hits per nine innings pitched and went 8–3. Hall of Famer Red Ruffing was the team's ace with 21 wins, and fellow Hall of Famer Lefty Gomez led the club in losses with just eight. The other five double-digit winners were Bump Hadley, Monte Pearson, Atley Donald, Steve Sundra, and Oral Hildebrand. Among the team's lesser contributors was another pitching great of the 1930s, Wes Ferrell, who won just a single game. The team scored 967 runs despite fielding a lineup that included a .233 hitter at shortstop and a first baseman who batted just .235. But the everyday lineup also featured three Hall of Famers and broke training camp with a fourth as a regular who was forced out of action permanently early in the season.

Name all six of these 1939 Yankees team members—the two subpar hitters, the three major offensive contributors, and the player expected to be a fourth major contributor who instead became a tragic loss.

Center fielder Joe DiMaggio, catcher Bill Dickey, second baseman Joe Gordon, and, of course, first baseman Lou Gehrig were the four Hall of Famer regulars when the season began. Frank Crosetti and Gehrig's first base replacement, Babe Dahlgren, toted the frail lumber.

What was the last of the 16 major-league franchises as of 1901 to suffer a last-place finish?

The 1952 Detroit Tigers, which finished 50–104, 14 games behind the 7th-place St. Louis Browns. In their previous 51 seasons the Tigers had seldom finished lower than the first division.

A team Triple Crown constitutes a team leading its league in batting average, ERA, and fielding average. Team Triple Crowns are rare indeed. Not even the 1939 Yankees won a team Triple Crown, finishing second to the Red Sox in batting average. Nor did the 1927 "Murderer's Row" Yankees club win one, finishing no better than in a three-way tie for third in fielding average. In all of major-league history, from 1871 forward, every team Triple Crown Winner has either won the pennant or qualified for postseason play by winning its division ... with two exceptions. In 1885, the New York Giants played .759 ball and won the team Triple Crown but nonetheless finished second in the National League, two games behind the Chicago White Stockings. For their trouble, the Giants earned nothing more than the highest winning percentage ever by an also ran. The only other team Triple Crown Winner to miss out on a pennant won the team batting title by 13 points, the fielding crown by four points, and posted a league best 2.09 ERA. With all that, this team finished five games behind the flag winner and two games back of the runner-up. Yes, that is correct. It finished in third place in an eight-team league, a record low by a team Triple Crown Winner. The only clues you should need to name that team is that it was managed by a future Hall of Famer that was never on a pennant winner and, two years later, under the same skipper, it set an all-time record for the closest finish by a runner-up to a flag winner in either the American or National League.

The 1906 Cleveland Naps, under player-manager Nap Lajoie and thanks largely to being terrible in one-run games and against lefty hurlers. Two years later the Naps lost the AL pennant to Detroit by half a game, the smallest losing margin ever by an American or National League runner-up.

Do you know the only team to bat around the order in the first inning of the first game of the first postseason series it ever appeared in, with all the damage coming after two outs?

It was the top of the very first inning in the very first "modern" World Series game. On October 1, 1903, playing at Boston's Huntington Avenue Grounds, the National League champion Pittsburgh Pirates burst out to a quick 4–0 lead against Boston's ace, Cy Young, in Game 1 after Young retired the first two batters and held on to win 7–3 behind Deacon Phillippe. It was the Pirates' first postseason appearance, although they had previously won pennants in both 1901 and 1902 before the NL and AL drafted a peace agreement enabling the two leagues to install a "World Series" at the close of regular-season play to determine an overall champion.

Arguably the best team in the Brooklyn–LA Dodgers long history won 104 games in a year when the schedule still called for only 154 games. The Dodgers that year nonetheless lost the flag by a two-game margin. The team that beat them out went on to win the World Series over a heavily favored opponent that featured the American League MVP who led the AL in just two batting departments—strikeouts and grounding into double plays. The National League batting leader that year, if today's rules had been in effect, would have been a .318 hitter on the NL flag winner rather than Ernie Lombardi, who won two. What season is under discussion here? Who were the two World Series opponents that year? Who was the AL MVP? Who would have won the NL batting crown according to current rules? And what is generally viewed as the main reason the Dodgers came up short of the pennant that season?

The year was 1942. The Cardinals beat the favored Yankees in the World Series. Yankees second baseman Joe Gordon was voted the AL MVP. Enos Slaughter posted the highest average in the NL among qualifiers as per current rules. Almost every Dodgers historian traces the club's failure to capture the 1942 flag to a July afternoon in St. Louis. The Dodgers had come into town on July 18 for back-to-back doubleheaders with an eight-game lead over the Cards and left with a six-game lead after Pete Reiser crashed into the center-field wall in the 11th inning of a 6–6 game chasing a long drive by Slaughter that ended up as a walk-off inside-the-park home run. Suffering from constant headaches, Reiser returned to action just six days later against doctors' advice to stay off the field until he was himself again and finished the season as barely a shadow of the player that had led the NL in batting and OPS in 1941, his first full big-league season. Reiser had a slash line of .350/.413/.520 prior to his head injury and was .244/.313/.367 the rest of the season to finish at .310/.375/.463. He was never again the same player.

What two teams finished the regular season in a lackluster 86–68 tie for the pennant that was decided by a best-of-three playoff? Their mutual .558 winning percentage prior to the playoff was the lowest ever by a team in first place at the close of a 154-game-schedule season. That year, the 7th-place Cardinals finished just 15 games out of first on closing day. Bobby Avila played second base for the losing team in the play-off series for the pennant. The batting leaders in both leagues hit over .350. Still need more clues? Cleveland played its last meaningful game in September for 36 years. Don't settle for less than the year, the two playoff teams, the two batting leaders, and the Tribe's out-of-nowhere sparkplug that season.

The year was 1959. In their second season in Los Angeles, the Dodgers swept the Milwaukee Braves in the three-game playoff for the National League pennant to finish with a .564 winning percentage. The batting champs were Hank Aaron (.355) and Harvey Kuenn (.353). Tito Francona, expected to add bench strength, instead took the Cleveland center-field job away from Jimmy Piersall and batted .363 but did not have enough plate appearances to wrestle the AL batting crown from Kuenn.

What team in 1945 had two hitters in the top three in batting in the AL that never played another major-league game? In fact, the only member of the club's regular infield to play another big-league game was its nineteen-year-old shortstop who lost his job the following year to a returning World War II vet who went on to make the Hall of Fame. Can you name the club, its two .300 hitters who dropped off the big-league map after 1945, and the future Hall of Famer?

The team was the Chicago White Sox. The two hitters among the top three batting leaders were outfielder Johnny Dickshot and third baseman Tony Cuccinello, who lost the American League batting title on the final day of the season to the Yankees' Snuffy Stirnweiss. Luke Appling was the future Hall of Famer. He reclaimed his shortstop post from Cass Michaels, a highly promising young player whose career mysteriously dissolved into mediocrity before it was abruptly derailed by a near fatal beaning in 1954. Dickshot and Cuccinello were both past thirty-five years of age by the time the 1945 season ended and had not seen regular duty in the majors for several seasons prior to that final wartime year.

What was the first team to win a World Championship with an infield that was comprised of four players who all produced 15 or more home runs? The club leader in homers was none other than its second baseman whose total set a league home run record at that position—one which lasted for over 50 years.

The 1948 Cleveland Indians, with Eddie Robinson (16) at first base, Joe Gordon (32) at second, Ken Keltner (31) at third, and Lou Boudreau (18) at shortstop. Gordon's 32 blasts remained the American League record for a second baseman until 2001 when Bret Boone hit 37 for the Seattle Mariners.

Name the only city to produce pennant-winning teams in three different leagues in the same decade. Your only clue is the reminder that 1900 was the final year of the nineteenth century.

The clue tells you that Boston's Players League pennant in 1890 occurred in the decade of the 1880s, and thus the city of Boston only had American Association (1891) and National League (1891–1893 and 1897–1898) pennant winners in the 1890s. On a different note, Brooklyn, a pennant winner in 1889, did not match up with New York Giants' and New York Mets' pennant winners also in the 1880s because Brooklyn was a separate city until 1898. The answer lies in the decade of the 1910s, which saw the Chicago Cubs win the NL flag in 1918, the White Sox win AL flags in 1917 and 1919, and the Federal League Chicago Whales triumph in 1915.

The Cleveland Indians broke an AL record set by the 2002 Oakland A's when they won their 21st-straight game on

September 13, 2017. The previous record of 19 that was bro-
ken by the A's was jointly held by two teams: the 1906 White
Sox and the 1947 Yankees. Several members of the 1906 Sox
were still alive when the 1947 Yanks tied their record, but only
one member of the 1947 Yankees was alive to see the Indians
set the current AL record, with 22 consecutive wins. Who is he?

Dr. Bobby Brown, who shared the Yankees' third base post in 1947 with Billy Johnson. Brown also is currently vying with Charlie Silvera for a record that was once held by Tommy Henrich: the first player to be the last surviving member of four different World Series winners prior to his death on December 1, 2009, at age ninety-six. If Brown outlives Silvera, he will be the last surviving member of five different World Series champs. However, if Silvera is the last man standing, he will be the last surviving member of no less than six different World Series winners! But Henrich holds a record that will always remain. On October 5, 1949, he became the first player to hit a solo walk-off home run in the bottom of the ninth inning in Game 1 of the World Series to win a 1–0 pitcher's duel between Allie Reynolds and Brooklyn's rookie ace, Don Newcombe.

Just once in major-league history prior to the inception of divi-
sion play has only one club in its league been above .500 as
late as August. Indeed, when the calendar turned to August
2 (roughly two-thirds of the way through the season) that club
stood at 67–34 with a .663 winning percentage and was 17
games ahead of the 2nd-place team in its league (which sported
a 51–52 record and was only 2 ½ games ahead of the 7th place
team! The 1st-place club will not be difficult to guess, but the
year may prove a challenge even to our expert historians. These

clues should help. As of August 1, the 7th-place club featured a slugger that had come to it in an earlier trade with the 1st-place club. His 38 home runs were double the amount of his team's home run runner-up who would go to the 1st-place club in a trade two years later and promptly win back-to-back MVP awards. Meanwhile, the 3rd-place club as of August 2 would go on to finish in 3rd place and feature the loop batting leader with a .328 mark, far below his career batting average. So... we're looking for three teams, three hitters, and the year in question.

The year was 1958. The 1st-place club, obviously the Yankees, played just .472 ball from August 2 on but still won the pennant by 10 games over the White Sox. The 3rd-place team, the Red Sox, featured Ted Williams, in an off year for him, who nevertheless won the batting crown with a .328 BA. The 7th-place club as of August 1 held on to 7th behind ex-Yankee Bob Cerv's booming bat that collected 38 home runs, double the amount hit by...well, a young Roger Maris. Who else could they be but the Kansas City A's, pejoratively known as the Yankees' major-league farm team in the late 1950s?

Of the 16 original major-league franchises extant at the beginning of the twentieth century, all but four team leaders in games played in their club's uniform are in the Hall of Fame. One is the Reds' Pete Rose, currently still on the Hall's ineligible list. A second, Derek Jeter, is not yet eligible for the Hall but a shoo-in once he is. Yet another is Bert Campaneris of the A's whom we've met elsewhere in these pages. The fourth, like Campaneris, spent the majority of his career at shortstop and was born more than 50 years earlier than Campy. His original team was the 1901 Pirates, and his final season came under Connie Mack in 1919. All of his other games came with his main team, where he served as a regular at both shortstop and third base at various junctures and never saw postseason action.

We could add that his main team had two different nicknames during the 15 seasons he served in its colors. The nicknames were the Naps and the Indians. His name was Terry Turner, with 1,619 games in a Cleveland uniform, five more than his longtime teammate Nap Lajoie.

What was the first season that two or more teams entered the final day of the campaign with a chance to win a major-league pennant? What were the teams, and which one won the flag?

On the morning of October 5, the final day of regular-season play in the 1889 National League, the Boston Beaneaters began the day with an 83–44 record pending the result of their game that afternoon at Pittsburgh. Starting for Boston was its ace, John Clarkson, who was shooting for his 50th victory against Pittsburgh's Jim Galvin. Meanwhile in Cleveland, the New York Giants awakened that morning with an 82–43 record pending the result of their game that afternoon that pitted their ace, Tim Keefe, against Cleveland's Henry Gruber. Both Clarkson and Keefe were expected to win, in which case New York would have won the pennant by three percentage points. Had New York lost, however, and Clarkson triumphed over Galvin, Boston would have won the flag by five percentage points. Galvin settled the issue by pitching a masterful game and denying not only Boston the pennant but Clarkson his 50th win. If Keefe had also lost to Gruber, New York would still have won the pennant by three percentage points. Since scoreboards were posted in major-league parks by 1889 that reflected events in other cities—as they came in by wire—it is likely that players on both contenders were scoreboard-watching even as their own games unraveled.

When the 1994 players strike hit all of MLB on August 12 and shut down the season, what team had the best record in the majors at 74–40? What other seven teams would have qualified for the playoffs if the season had closed the day of the strike, and why was it the first season there would have been as many as eight postseason qualifiers?

Montreal had the best record on the day the door slammed shut on the strike-shortened season. The seven other postseason qualifiers would have been the Reds, Astros, and Dodgers in the National League, and the Yankees, White Sox, Indians, and Rangers in the American League. There were eight qualifiers for the first time because each league had divided into three divisions prior to the 1994 season and added a wild card—the non-division winner with the best record. In the NL, that would have been Houston, and Cleveland would have been the AL wildcard. Texas, at 52–62 on closing day, owned the best record in the AL West division and would have become the second postseason entrant to date with a losing record had there been a postseason. Montreal, meanwhile, would have concluded the season for the lone time in its history as a major-league franchise with the top record in the majors. Would it also have emerged with its only pennant? Alas, we'll never know.

But do you know the only team to date with a losing record to take part in postseason play?

The 1981 Kansas City Royals, winners of the American League West in the second half of the only season split into two parts owing to a midseason players' walkout. The Royals finished seven games over .500 in the second half after finishing 10 below in the first half for a composite 50–53 record.

What was the most recent World Series entrant to get at least seven innings from each of its four starters?

The 2005 Chicago White Sox, who swept the Astros in four straight games behind John Garland, Mark Buehrle, Freddy Garcia, and Jose Contreras.

What National League team began the twentieth century by finishing in 2nd place in its league despite having a regular shortstop that hit .194, a regular second baseman that hit .187, and a regular center fielder that posted a .334 slugging average, a full 20 points below its future Hall of Fame team batting leader who finished at .354? The team had yet to win its first pennant even though it had been a member of the National League since 1883.

The 1901 Phillies finished at 83–57 and 7½ games behind the pennant-winning Pirates despite carrying two sub-.200 hitters in its middle infield, shortstop Monte Cross and second baseman Bill Hallman, and center fielder Roy Thomas who collected just eight extra-base hits. Ed Delahanty, the Phillies' batting leader that year in almost every major category, jumped to the American League in 1902, along with several of its pitchers, and the club slid all the way to 7th place. It would not contend again for over a decade.

What American League team won 103 games on a schedule that called for a maximum of 154 games but was nonetheless eliminated from contention on September 18 with more than a week still left in the season? One clue should be enough. The team's Hall of Fame manager posted his top winning percentage as a skipper that season.

The 1954 Yankees, under Casey Stengel, went 103–51, the only time a Stengel-led team won more than two-thirds of its games. However, they finished second to the Indians, which registered 111 wins and an American League–record .721 winning percentage.

Only once in major-league history has a team finished its season with the most wins in its league and yet failed to win the pennant. What was the team, and what were the circumstances that led to it becoming a runner-up?

Going into the final day of the 1915 Federal League season, the Chicago Whales, Pittsburgh Rebels, and St. Louis Terriers were separated by a scant few percentage points, but St. Louis had nonetheless been mathematically eliminated because Chicago and Pittsburgh were slated to play a doubleheader, with the pennant going to Pittsburgh if it won both games and to Chicago if it either won both or split the pair. Chicago won the pennant by a single percentage point over St. Louis and a half game over Pittsburgh when the doubleheader was split. The irony was that St. Louis won the most games (87) because it was the only one of the three teams to play a full 154-game schedule. Following so close on the heels of the 1908 American League race that was also decided by games with not having to be made up despite having possible bearing on the pennant race, it would seem the 1915 Federal League fiasco would once and for all spark the installation of a rule that would require such make-up games to be played. But this was still not the case. In 1938, the National League pennant could have gone to Pittsburgh rather than Chicago if both teams had been required to make up missing games, and as late as the 1950 season there was still no rule to extend the season beyond the scheduled closing date unless a pennant race ended in a flatfooted tie. There now is, since 1994, not only to decide the division winners but also to determine wild-card spots.

All the baseball historians who would have it that the 2017 Minnesota Twins are the first team ever to make it into postseason play the season after losing 100 or more games the previous season are not really worthy of calling themselves true baseball historians. Why are they not?

In 1890, after finishing dead last in the American Association the previous season with a record of 27–111 for an abysmal .196 winning percentage, the Louisville Cyclones rallied under their new manager Jack Chapman to become the first major-league team to go from worst to first when they took the AA pennant by a 10-game margin over the Columbus Solons. This earned them the right to play Brooklyn in the final World's Series between the National League and AA pennant winners. The series ended in a 3–3 tie that was called a draw owing to poor weather and even poorer attendance.

Since each of the two major leagues divided into three divisions in 1994, what is the only team—prior to the 2018

Yankees—to collect more than 100 wins in the regular season and fail to win its division?

It's already been nearly two decades since the Seattle Mariners cruised to the AL West division title by tying the 1906 Chicago Cubs' record of 116 wins, yet the Mariners are still looking for their first pennant. Second to the Mariners in 2001 were the Oakland A's who finished with 102 wins, including a then AL-record 21 victories in a row that has since been broken by the 2017 Indians. The A's incidentally were not only second to the Mariners in the AL West that year—they had the second-best record in the majors but lost in the first round of the playoffs to the AL East champion Yankees.

What team recently fell one home run short of being the first team in National League history to feature six players with 25 or more home runs but nonetheless finish last in its division? Name the only two batting title qualifiers on the team that hit fewer than 24 home runs.

The 2017 Cincinnati Reds, last in the NL Central. Center fielder Billy Hamilton and utilityman Jose Peraza hit fewer than 24 home runs, while shortstop Zack Cozart finished with 24.

Under the present postseason format—excluding ties—what is the maximum number of games a team can play in a single postseason?

Hope you didn't say 21. The answer is 23 if there is a three- or four-way tie for the second wild-card spot and even more in the remote chance that more than four teams were to tie. The breakdown max is: World Series = 7; LCS = 7; DCS = 5; and WC = at minimum 1 and at maximum 12.

In the 24-year span between 1969 and 1993 when each major league went right to a League Championship Series between the two division winners to determine which of the two would represent its league in the World Series, what was the only team to play in five consecutive League Championship Series?

The 1971–1975 Oakland A's, still the only team to win three consecutive World Championships under more than one manager. Dick Williams piloted the 1972–1973 A's champs, and Alvin Dark was at the helm of the 1974 club. Ironically, the A's had their best regular-season records during that span in 1971 and 1975, the two years they lost the ALCS to the Orioles and Red Sox, respectively.

*5***** The 1902 Pirates were the last team to win 100 or more games in a season before the schedule was increased from 140 to 154 games in 1904. What is the only American League team to win 100 games in a season when the schedule called for fewer than 154 games? The only clue that should be needed here is that extenuating circumstances caused the regular-season schedule to be abbreviated.*

Right, the extenuating circumstances were that a war was going on—but not in the traditional sense. The war was between the players and the owners, and because peace terms were not reached after the 1994 strike until the spring of 1995, the regular season could not commence until April 25, forcing a schedule reduction from 162 games to 144. Despite the 18-game reduction,

Cleveland logged 100 victories on the head to capture the AL Central with a 100–44 mark and a .694 winning percentage.

Conclusion

WHERE TO RATE YOURSELF AMONG TRIVIA EXPERTS?

Well, nobody's going to believe you if you profess that you batted 1.000 on the 200+ questions in this book…even .750 is a stretch.

But something in the neighborhood of .600, with 5 hits awarded on each at-bat on the 5-star questions that follow each section in the book, puts you in the company of the elite baseball trivia players active today.

Actually, you'd be a welcome addition to almost any team and a fearsome challenger in individual competitions.

Truth be told, you're ready to test your mettle among the best of the best if you bat .300 so long as you were able to nail at least a smattering of questions from all eras of the game, ranging from 1871 to 2018.